S0-AFV-693

WE LIKE IT WILD

WE LIKE IT WILD

by Bradford Angier

COLLIER BOOKS

Macmillan Publishing Company

NEW YORK

COLLIER MACMILLAN PUBLISHERS

LONDON

Macmillan Publishing Company
866 Third Avenue, New York, N.Y. 10022
Collier Macmillan Canada, Inc.

We Like It Wild was originally published in a hardcover edition by Stackpole Books and is reprinted by arrangement.

First Collier Books Edition 1973

Library of Congress Catalog Card Number: 63-18278

ISBN: 0-02-097200-8

12 11 10 9 8 7

Macmillan books are available at special discounts for bulk purchases for sales promotions, premiums, fund-raising, or educational use. For details, contact:

    Special Sales Director
    Macmillan Publishing Company
    866 Third Avenue
    New York, N.Y. 10022

Printed in the United States of America

For Vena,
who made the wilderness home.

Contents

WE LIKE IT WILD

1

A Walk in the Boston Snow

Thin distant cheeps of migrating birds caught at us, along with subarctic cold, as we stepped into the British Columbia night. Wild wings flapped nearer. Raucous cries, mingling vaguely with the insistence of slush that gave a pewter gleam to the river, all at once emphasized the smells of approaching winter.

Suddenly, an uneven angle hyphened itself against a sky tremulous with Northern Lights. Wild swan! Spellbound after too many years in cities. Vena and I stood together and watched the great swift shapes until they chalked out of sight.

A timber wolf began howling in one of the dry canyons across the Peace River. The answering bark of our dog was engulfed when the whole pack joined in, so close that the pandemonium seemed to come from no particular direction but to sound stereophonically all around the clearing. In the wind-heaving stillness that followed, a coyote yipped in the hills behind us.

Bushman began barking again inside the cabin, his body making leaping shadows in the light from the window. Only then did I realize that snow was beginning to swirl in our faces. Big soft flakes, heavy as damp feathers, eddied after us into the suddenly wonderful warmth of our log home.

"Sorry?" Vena asked. "Sorry we're here with all the food, wood, and all the everything else we'll need all winter?"

"Sure, I'm sorry," I said, one hand around her and the other stroking the Irish wolfhound's grey head. "I'm sorry we didn't make the break a lot sooner."

Food, warmth, clothing, and shelter: the four necessities. Vena and I had them all, plus such luxuries as saddle horses in the nearby pole corral and shelves piled high with books there was time to read. Especially important here, we had each other. Glancing through the sifting whiteness at where lamp light glistened on stacks of poplar and split pine, I stirred the fire with more satisfaction than ever.

Most of my life, up to now, I had never been fully happy because I'd always wanted to be somewhere else. But, then, isn't this same urge experienced by millions? We all hope some day to answer it. In most cases, however, it keeps opening a deeper and wider void all our lives. My own trouble had been that the quest had kept leading me in what was, for me at least, precisely the wrong direction; toward big cities.

There is one thing I wish I had realized sooner. It's that too many of us are working harder than we want, at things we don't like to do. Why? So as to afford the sort of existence we don't care to live.

Just for instance, how about you? Would you rather live where wild fruits and vegetables are free for the gathering, trout for the fishing, steak for the hunting, fuel for the cutting, and a home for the satisfaction of building?

So would we. The only difference between us and a lot of others, as a matter of fact, is that this is exactly what we seem to be doing.

I'd put off going for a long while. It had seemed the only sensible course to follow. At least, that was what everyone said. There were such things as career, making a living, and other responsibilities. I went over them all again that grey January day in Boston, where I was editor of an amusement business weekly.

The brick buildings looked old and smoky as I crossed Gloucester Street, and I don't suppose I should have been surprised when a passing taxi drenched my trouser legs, for other cars had swerved around the corner with such fervor that slush pocked the powdering of snow on the brownstone steps behind me. Wind hit when I reached the Esplanade. Anyway, I thought, there would be no automobiles here. Then a horn sounded, and I jumped. A police sedan passed down the concrete path, printing a muddy track.

Snow was getting down my neck even though I turned up the collar of my topcoat. Drab ribbons of mist were heavy over the dark dampness of the Charles River, and trees thrusting themselves up near the bank angled shadows over an uneasy surface. Lines of automobiles jerked nervously up and down Commonwealth Avenue to my right. Although the traffic's frenzy was hushed by the snowfall, it was as unnerving as ever. This is what millions of people were settling for. This was what I was settling for.

I had just come back from a four-week trip along the wilderness headwaters of the Southwest Miramichi River in New Brunswick, and I appreciated more than ever what scientists meant when they said that human beings were intended to spend most of their hours beneath open skies. The city had a sodden, helpless look which the increasing wetness of my feet didn't brighten. It wasn't as if there weren't hundreds of thousands of miles that haven't even been walked on yet—where, at bargain basement prices, one can stretch and breathe and really live.

Yet crowded, complaining millions continue to make themselves sick in their unhappy hysteria to lay up something against a sick day. Their incessant anxiety and strain is a well-nigh uncurable form of disease. When they aren't feverishly wondering how to get away from the city, I thought, they're cursing the chains that drag them back. Like me, I thought.

Most of what the government doesn't take, they spend in trying to live up to the other fellow. I considered how many families I knew around Boston who would be needlessly poor all their lives because they thought they must live in a house or apartment like their neighbors. Thinking back to my trip, I realized that before it became unfashionable, a comfortable home was built on this continent almost entirely of such materials as nature furnishes ready to hand.

The usually hazy atmosphere was cleaner than usual because of the falling snow. But when I turned between dirty drifts toward Beacon Street, a twisting gust of cold wind brought, along with a muddy smell from the Charles River, a mixture of exhaust fumes and railroad smoke.

Now that I go back over it in my mind, I can remember every yard of that walk downtown. But while I was actually walking it, I forgot to take the right turn on Arlington Street that would have led me by the Ritz Carlton and the Statler to the film district and my office. Instead, I went on, past children playing in the snow by the frozen Frog Pond, almost all the way to the red brick State House with its incongruous marble wings. I had to cut back across Boston Common.

Twitching elm trees made a pattern of advertising signs on Boylston Street. The wind, rawer than I remembered it in the woods where I'd been better dressed and more warmly disposed, didn't help my outlook any. Even the wind, I thought, was halfway free which was more than could be said for me.

A blast of warm air from a drugstore made me realize how uncomfortable my wet feet were in their low city shoes. Ahead, the lights of the Metropolitan Theatre were a warm glow. By virtue of my job, I had a pass there. Now that I'd started thinking so seriously, maybe it would be just as well to sit in the heated darkness awhile and try to get things straight. For example, perhaps a transfer to the West Coast, with its new faces and different scenes, would solve everything.

It was in the theatre that one of those small things happened that, although scarcely touching you at all, can change the whole trend of your existence. I was sitting there, and watching the picture which I can't remember, when a man started up the aisle. His step was unsteady. I thought, maybe when he was my age he'd wanted to go to the woods, too, and had also kept putting it off. Then he passed my seat, and I saw he was very old. If he ever did have those dreams, I thought, now it was too late.

My luncheon date with Vena was in one of those little eating places below the sidewalk level of Newbury Street. I had seen her first when she was dancing in ballet. Now, not wanting to go on the road again, she was producing musical shows for a theatre a short drive outside of town. Perhaps it was the candlelight, but she seemed to be dancing now as she came across the room, slim ankles and high heels beneath a long fur coat catching the daylight from the doorway. I got up and held a chair for her, and she settled into it and flung open her coat in one graceful moment.

"I want to marry you," Vena says I said abruptly.

"Why, I want to marry you, too," Vena says she said.

"I don't mean it quite that way. I mean, there's something else I have to do. Everyone all my life has been telling me it's just a phase that will pass; that it's something I can be working toward for my old age instead of wasting time on it now when I should be making money."

That was it exactly, except that all at once I no longer saw any sense in spending the best years of my life earning money in order to enjoy a questionable liberty during the least valuable part.

"You want to try living in the woods," she said.

"Perhaps it won't work out. Perhaps I won't like it. But even then, don't you see, I can come back, and nothing will have been lost except a little time. At worst, I'll have had the sort of experience I've never been able to get enough of."

She nodded slowly.

"Otherwise," I said, "even if I'm wrong, there'd always be that hunger eating away. There'd always be the doubt."

Someone must have come in, for the candle on our table started flickering. I remember thinking how it glowed on Vena's sober, intense face like spring moonlight sifting through blossoms. I hadn't felt so alive in weeks.

"Don't you see?" I asked. "Then, no matter what, I'll know."

"Of course, I see," she said.

"It's no good just to keep on thinking about it. I'll never be any younger or more ready. Why should I mind what others think? They don't have the same drives. That's proved by the different things they like, even here in the city. Besides, they're looking at it the wrong way."

"What wrong way?" she asked.

"You know the theory. Civilized life is complicated and difficult. Wilderness life is simple. Complex things are not as easy to handle as simple things. Therefore, the man who deliberately escapes the difficult in favor of the easy is inferior, out of adjustment, lazy. The point is that the city life, where you have nearly everything done for you in exchange for some one job on your part, is the easy one."

There was a silence before she answered, as if she were thinking. "I don't know much about it," she said. "I've never lived outside of cities."

"You see, there's far more to it than that theory. This desire people in all ages have always had to return to the primitive places is something they're born with.

It's the same sort of racial urge that makes some birds fly south in the fall." I drew a deep breath. "I've got to go this time, Vena."

"Well," she said slowly. Then she smiled, and her quickness returned. "When do we leave?"

"We?"

"Unless you'd rather go alone."

"No, but this time—."

"What's so special about this time?" she asked.

"It's apt to be rough, Vena. I thought that I could try it by myself first."

She didn't say anything.

"Then if it worked out and if I could get a place ready for us," I said, "well, if you were still willing—. Well, I hoped you might not mind waiting until then."

"Don't you suppose girls have racial instincts, too?" she asked, looking at me in the half-light of the room. "And, as you said, if it doesn't work out, we can always come back."

"A year?" I asked, taking the hand she reached across the table.

"A year should make a nice, reasonable honeymoon."

"Then we can decide," I said. "We'll come back in a year, anyway, if you say. I'll take a leave of absence, and it'll be entirely up to you."

2

Train North of the Hub

There's always the same indefinable excitement at the memory of how, after rumbling slowly backwards until stopping with a clanging jolt, the train started forward. A series of gradually diminishing jerks lengthened into a smooth succession of clacks. We were finally on our way.

In a sense, the behavior of the train was not unlike our own experience after that candlelit decision on Newbury Street. So little seemed to happen at first that for a long time we had the feeling of going backwards.

The hardest part of taking to the woods is getting started. At times our progress was so slow that it must have seemed to Vena that we weren't really going at all. I still wasn't sure what she really thought about this rerouting of our lives. I wasn't even any longer certain how I felt about it myself. But, then, we would have a year in which to find out.

The locomotive punctuated its plunge through the New England night with a series of shrieks. Pellets of early February snow stung frosting windows. Softer flakes eddied after the cars. Signal lights, somewhere in the deepening cold outside, reflected on Vena's face

which looked white and strained. Then she smiled, and
everything was all right.

"I wonder how he's taking all this?" she said.

It took me a minute to realize what she was talking
about.

"Let's go see," I said.

Bushman, oxford grey head couched watchfully on
large paws, was curled in the farthest corner of the
baggage car. His muzzled nose extended cautiously.
Then a grey length of tail gave a tentative flick. The
next moment he was jumping at the end of a short
leash, and the tail was flailing.

"Down," I said, although it didn't do any good.

"Yours?" the baggageman asked. When I nodded, he
went on, "Big dog. The fellows are leery of him."

"He's just a pup. Six months old."

"Him? He weighs an even hundred pounds."

"He'll weigh nearly twice that when he's grown."

"Him?" the baggageman said again. "If you're looking for his food, Lady, I guess that's it in that burlap
bag. The water's in the corner back there. I was about
to get to it. What kind of a dog is he, anyway? I guess I
never saw another one."

"He's an Irish wolfhound." I stroked the long, wiry
coat. Bushman's amber eyes were on Vena, however,
and I remember wondering if he was already learning
that women are the practical ones of this world.
"They're the tallest, although not the heaviest, dogs. I
never saw one, either, until I bought him."

A glance behind Dhulart dun Delgan, which was his
registered name, reminded me that the companionship
of the large grey puppy was not the only essential we
had secured for the trip north. Six duffle bags, their
contents the product of many hours, bulged against
the wall.

The train shrieked through a station where another
train was standing. For a moment, it was as if each of
the amber rectangles bobbing past the narrow windows

of the baggage car door was registering one more item
we had painstakingly added to our outfit. In a way, I
thought, that had proved the answer to getting started.
Once you have reached your decision, you begin by
getting together an outfit.

"Why are you staring at those bags with such an odd
expression?" Vena asked me.

"What?" I said. "Oh, I was wondering if we'd
brought everything we'll need."

She glanced from the eating Bushman to the heap of
canvas sacks. Then she turned toward me. Her forehead smoothed, and it was as if there was no one else;
as if, for the moment, the solar system was holding its
breath and there was no one abroad but us, no one in
harmony with the rhythm of the universe but us
two.

"I don't know about you," she said, and I remember
being surprised at the strength in her small hand.

The temperature was still falling outside. Snow stung
at our faces when we steadied ourselves through the
passageways between the cars. From a vestibule window we could see locomotive smoke forming a heavy
haze. Some of its electrifying odor seeped into the
creaking passage.

The moon had come out. The countryside it shone
on was naked and frozen. The sight of it somehow
drained my self-assurance until I didn't seem to have
anything left but a queer feeling in my stomach. In
Boston, spurred on by an atavistic urge, and caught
up in the whirl of planning and buying and of writing
to places I'd never been and to people I'd never met,
for days I hadn't had time to think.

Now I wondered what I was doing here on this
hurtling mass of metal, plunging away from everything
I knew and could surely cope with, being borne relent-
lessly toward the frozen edge of space. How could I,
who had lived in cities all my life, ever hope to contend
with the savage demands of survival back of beyond?

And suppose the experiment failed? Would we be left stranded when our money was gone? How could I ever have let myself involve Vena in such a reckless venture?

Some horses in a rolling pasture were racing beside the train. We both must have seen them at the same time because we each started to speak. In another instant they were left far behind, and we looked at each other and laughed. I felt a loneliness in myself rush out in that moment to embrace what must have been a similar loneliness in her, and suddenly the world was right again.

"Hungry?" I asked, holding the door for her.

"Sleepy. It's been a long day. Why, are you hungry?"

"No," I said. "It's been a long time, but now we're on our way."

"Yes," she said, "nothing's going to stop us now."

"That's right," I said. "At least, we'll be able to give it our try."

One of the pitfalls in life is that you're apt to keep telling yourself there is lots of time. Time, I thought that next morning in Montreal, was much like the train the night before, sometimes moving rapidly, then slowly, and occasionally even backing as if to gather its resources. Now that we were finally on our way to somewhere we'd never been within 2,000 miles of before, and to a sort of life we had never led, I realized what a big step I'd taken and how easy it would have been to keep on telling myself there was plenty of time.

Whenever there was a long enough stop during the transcontinental journey, we unhooked Bushman's leash and walked him back and forth beside the cars. From Edmonton, the continent's northernmost large city, we boarded the last of our trains, made sure Bushman was snug, and settled down to jolting northward a fifth night and day.

"I thought we'd be in the mountains by now," Vena said.

"So did I."

The landscape, when in the late sunrise we could see it again, continued to be flat and monotonous. The main point of interest, in fact, proved to be how the snow on both sides of the right of way was heavy with tracks. Rabbits were at the peak of their cycle, the porter explained.

"Do you mean rabbits did all that?" Vena asked.

"Varying hares, actually, Ma'am. They almost die out. Then about every ten years they come back by the millions and gnaw everything they can reach. About the time everyone hereabouts is near tired to death of rabbit stew, they die off again."

Dawson Creek, British Columbia, when we finally reached the end of the steel in the late afternoon, was little more than a couple of muddy main streets with high board sidewalks. A tank wagon was delivering water to the few cabins, and two steaming horses were having a hard time of it. We found a hotel across from the station, left Bushman with the baggageman until we could arrange to have him and the luggage picked up, and looked for a place to eat. There were still no mountains.

The countryside, stubbled with brush and deeply cut by streams, remained depressingly flat and rolling until, crowded into the cab of a truck, we went through the even smaller town of Fort St. John the next day and turned left up the north bank of the Peace River. Bushman was riding behind, tied atop a load of freight for the Indian Department.

"Look," Vena said, and she sat more erect.

Gooseflesh raised between my shoulders. A white mass of mountain, with a roundness that made it seem more companionable than austere, reared dramatically against the cloud-streaked sky.

"Bullhead Mountain," the driver said. "Hudson

Hope is right below it, although, strange enough, you can't see Bullhead from there."

The western sky later cleared between clouds and horizon, and we could make out a white sea of peaks glistening in the sunset. But, for me, it was still Bullhead Mountain that dominated the scene.

The tawny clay under our tires began to freeze in the early Northern evening. As the multiple rear wheels spun up the stony grade lifting from the deep cottonwood shade of a creek, the truck skidded toward the sheer drop at the left. I slumped back self-consciously, as a rut straightened us out. The driver, gearing down, swapped me a grin for my sheepish look.

"This isn't much of a road," he said, "but only a few years ago there was no way into Hudson Hope at all except by river and by horse trail. After all, it's about 140 miles from the end of the railroad. But they're getting coal out of Bullhead again, and there had to be some way for the trucks to get in."

"Didn't I read somewhere that an old coal mine near some dinosaur tracks had closed down?" Vena said.

"The old mine on the river is closed," the driver said. "That's where Alexander Mackenzie discovered coal back in 1793 when he became the first man to cross the main North American continent. Mackenzie went upriver right past here. Wintered not far below Hudson Hope."

"You mean there's another mine now?" I asked.

"Yes, King Gething started another one part way up the side of Bullhead. I'll be getting a load of coal from there on the trip out."

Bushman's barking sounded from the squeaking load behind.

"He hears them," the driver said, flicking a hand toward the hard bright ribbon of river below. Dark specks were moving from an island that was dark with spruce. "Coyotes. We'll be traveling the ice there a ways."

I expected the ride to become smooth after we eased down the bank, but there was a continuous jolting. Through the driver's open door I could hear a creaking and cracking that did not seem to be coming from the truck. The ice gave the impression of bending elastically beneath our weight. I looked at Vena. She smiled back at me in a strained sort of way.

"Better have your door open, too," the driver said. "Then there'll be time, in case we do go through, for the two of you to jump free."

A flurry of snow began flattening against the windshield. When the bank loomed ahead of us, it was as if the driver could see just far enough ahead to avoid trees that appeared as through raw cotton. The engine roared. Then I could feel familiar ruts cradling the wheels once more.

"Not far now," the driver said. "Staying with anyone in particular?"

"The hotel."

"Will that be out of your way?" Vena asked.

"No, that's where I'll be eating and sleeping, too, as soon as I get this load in the Bay's warehouse."

The air had cleared again. Below us, a sparse handful of lights suddenly twinkled. We swept among several dark bulges that must have been cabins. Toward the left was a clearing upon which several buildings silhouetted themselves on the river bank. The truck headed toward another small cluster of cabins, then swerved in an ice-crunching arc to draw up in front of a compact two-story structure with a wide porch. The headlights caught a sign long enough for me to read: Hudson Hope Hotel.

Cold, laced with the redolence of wood fires, immersed me as I stepped carefully into frozen ruts and crusted snow. I look curiously around, but already Vena was following, and I reached up both hands to steady her.

Up under the tarpaulin that was a dark bulge over

the load, Bushman was barking. I could see the driver throwing back the folds of canvas. Despite the fact that the truck motor was still throbbing, and although somewhere in the darkness other dogs had joined the racket, wind-swollen stillness seemed to encompass us.

I felt a great inward peace, stirred as the wind stirred the night by a sense of exhilaration. This was the real wilderness. Now if we could only find our niche somewhere in it.

The hotel door opened, and the briskness of cooking joined the other smells.

"Better come in where it's warm," a voice said. I couldn't remember ever having heard a friendlier sound. "Mrs. Ferguson is about to put out supper."

"Right you are, Bob," called back the driver.

3

Land for the Finding

The sensation of well-being persisted the next morning. I had a sense of peace and richness and excitement; a zest for living I couldn't remember ever having felt before. It was like groping up a mountain, and there, just ahead in the first sunshine seen for eons, suddenly is the top.

The world was a dark immensity when I awoke. Stars pricked the sky like bright icicle points. Moonlight gave a sheen to the snow about the window, making the northern night satiny and sequinned. Vena, still untouched by it all, was curled so quietly that I tried not to disturb her. Finally, even though the darkness remained as deep as midnight, I couldn't stay in bed any longer.

The upstairs room was on the southeast corner of the log hotel. To the east, the road down which we'd come was two shining ruts. Across a snowy expanse to the south loomed a squarish white building with a long sign above its plate glass windows. Feeling for woolen shirt and trousers, I made out—*Hudson's Bay Company*.

The buildings of the nearly 300-year-old company, oldest trading corporation in the world, were neatly tied together by a white picket fence. From the lower windows of what must have been the dwelling, light cut yellow rectangles from the night. Then I saw other light coming from the hotel kitchen.

Holding my watch so that I could make out its luminous hands, I saw the time was nearly nine o'clock. Here, near the top of the world, what I had taken to be the middle of the night was really the North's prolonged winter darkness.

I don't remember now what I had for breakfast, but I suppose it was eggs, for Mrs. Ferguson had a reputation for omelets. I do recall that the meal, ready when I came in from feeding Bushman, tasted a whole lot better than breakfast ever had in the city.

The thermometer by the front door showed ten below zero. The air, however, didn't feel as cold as Boston in a damp east wind with the temperature thirty degrees higher. The rubber-bottomed leather boots, heavy woolen sox, cotton shorts, and woolen trousers, shirt, light jacket, and mitts were what I ordinarily wore when hunting in Maine and the Maritimes. They were plenty warm now.

"Greetings," someone said, and whoever it was put a burr in the word.

A figure was standing at a gate in the white picket fence I'd observed from the window. There didn't seem to be anyone else about.

"Hello," I said and turned that way.

"That's considerable animal you have." The man nodded at Bushman who was bounding among the ruts, sawdust still clinging to his coat from the ante-room of the log ice house in which he had slept. "How is he on a sled?"

"Well," I said, "I guess he'd ride on one all right."

"Guess he would, at that," the man said after a moment, and he chuckled.

"Here, Bushman," I called. "Actually, he's only a few days older than six months. I'd like to train him later to carry a pack, at least."

The wolfhound, who was being scrutinized by a bristling, little, yellow dog, bounced over to us. I scratched his wiry back, while the man rubbed a velvety ear. I could see that the stranger wore an ordinary tweed suit with a sweater beneath it. On his head was a glossy hat of marten fur, wedge shaped like an oversize overseas cap.

"My name is Dave Cuthill," the man said. "I'm manager here for the Hudson's Bay Company. I answered your inquiry."

"Yes," I said, "of course. Thank you, Mr. Cuthill."

"The name is Dave," he said. "Glad to write. It's a treat to talk to someone new if only by post. We've been wondering if you have decided on a place yet."

"Well, no," I said. "You mentioned a cabin hereabouts, Dave."

"Yes, Fred Gaylor has one that he told me he'd be happy to have you use. No charge."

"We'd want to pay something if we lived in it."

"You'd have to fix it up some. That would be more than pay enough." Dave Cuthill motioned at a building partially hidden among shrubbery where, just before the hotel, the road from Fort St. John branched and part of it slanted up the hill above the town. "Fred's the telegraph operator across there. His cabin is a sort of summer one, upriver a mile."

"It's beside the river, then?"

"Yes. The only thing is, it's on a sheer cut bank. You couldn't get down to the Peace for about a mile on either side."

"Oh," I said. "we were planning to spend quite a bit of time on the Peace."

"I guess there are drawbacks to almost everything," Dave said. "Dudley Shaw has a cabin near it you could have, but he'd want it when he comes to work here again in the summer. He ordinarily lives above three miles above the Hope. You ought to talk to Dudley, anyway."

"Do I take the same road upriver?"

"There's only the one road on this flat."

"How about what looks like a road up the hill there?"

"Oh," Dave Cuthill said, "that's the portage. It goes around the north side of Bullhead Mountain. The river twists south of Bullhead; only Rocky Mountain Canyon where the river runs is twenty-two miles long, and it's unnavigable. The portage cuts the distance in two. There's a road off it up Bullhead to King Gething's coal mine."

Something had attracted Bushman's attention. He ducked under my hand.

"The dogs around here won't bother a pup any," Dave said. "Sounds as if someone is coming this way."

"Are there any good cabin sites across the portage?"

"There's cabin sites and empty cabins everywhere in the Northwest. The only thing is, Brad, you've already gotten away from civilization. Anywhere you head off a trail now is wilderness. Why pick a place where you'll have to spend unnecessary time packing mail and supplies? If I were you, the Canyon is where I'd pick."

A homemade sleigh, unpainted and substantial, was grating and squeaking along the road. The iron shoes of the two horses, one brown and the other white, struck musically against ice and crusted snow. The small yellow dog I'd seen previously was circling the team. When Bushman tried to renew his acquaintance, the yellow dog growled at him threateningly. A round man, with merry round eyes and unruly black hair that a stocking cap tossed only more askew, bulged comfortably on a plank that slanted across the sides.

"This is Ted Boynton," Dave said when the round man hopped down, and Ted smiled as he shoved out a stubby hand. "Brad Angier, Ted. He was wondering about that trail up the Canyon."

"Glad to meet you, Brad," Ted said. He was wearing blue overalls, and his flannel shirt was open at the throat. "Why, now, the trail was all right the last time I was up that way for wood. I guess Dudley is keeping it open."

"Dudley Shaw is the old-timer I told you about," Dave said. "He clerks for me summers. Winters he traps mink, fisher, lynx, beaver, and such up in the Canyon. You'll want to stop in and see him if you walk upriver."

"He may not be up," Ted Boynton said. "Dud lives pretty much by the sun."

"Then you can stop in on the way back. Are those cabins up by Bull Creek still in good shape, Ted? I guess you know Brad is looking for a place where he and his wife can settle. That spot up there would give them seasoned logs, at least."

"The fires haven't gotten in there," Ted said, adjusting his stocking cap. "I reckon the logs are still there for the taking. No one owns anything up that way, nobody does, except for one quarter section. Poor land for crops or grazing."

"They're just looking for a place to live," Dave said. "If they like it, could you run their outfit the five miles up there by sleigh for, say, five dollars?"

"Yes, sir," Ted said heartily. "For just living, I reckon there isn't any prettier spot around."

Every place, large or small, that comes to mean something to you takes on a personality of its own. Hudson Hope's as far as I was involved, sprang into life for me that first morning. There was the aroma of lodgepole pine and spruce and poplar, sharpened by the keenness of wood smoke. There was the peacefulness of a sleepy little settlement of perhaps two dozen log buildings, clustered about the H.B.C. outpost that bought its services and purchased its furs, at the same time supplying most of its store food and the majority of its goods.

Lamp light, here and there, streamed tawnily into the blueness of approaching dawn. Dogs lunged out of the shadows at Bushman whose puppyhood proved to be his defense. Then, before I realized it, I was beyond the town and walking along a high, river-bordering flat. I saw the cabin Mr. Gaylor had been kind enough to offer us. Other dark buildings bulged nearer the cut bank, but I did not stop to investigate.

Bushman's thoughts were occupied, too. Varying hare were everywhere. So was Bushman. The long-legged animals zigzagged so erratically that he invariably overran them. Far from discouraging him, this seemed only to arouse both temper and determination. Watching him, I wondered how I was ever going to overcome this instinct sufficiently to turn him into a practical packdog.

It wasn't until I passed Dudley Shaw's still dark main cabin some two miles further along that the wilderness, along with the renewed sharpness of wood smoke, really caught at me. Tremendous spruce and the biggest poplar I'd ever seen so shaded the ground that the undergrowth was sparse as in a park. There was scarcely a movement except for fragments of wind in the boughs; hardly a sound but for distant open water and the almost imperceptible swish of high air.

Then Bushman was barking. I saw a small man coming down the trail with big snowshoes angled like wings over bony shoulders. Thick-lensed glasses gleamed beneath the brim of a nearly shapeless felt hat.

"Here, Bushman," I said.

But the dog continued to run and to bark. Then he stopped doing both and stood well to one side in the snow, nose extended in discreet inquiry.

"Cheerio," the small man said in a voice that was not at all small. "I thought you'd be rambling up this way one day soon. You must be Brad."

"That's right," I said. "But I just got here last night."

"Moccasin telegraph," the small man said cheerfully.

"A stranger is vast doings in a jungle like this. My name is Shaw. Folks call me Dudley."

"Hello," I said. Bushman, who'd approached gingerly, was sniffing the stranger's outstretched fingers and flicking an oxford grey tail. "I've heard of you."

"Small world," Dudley said approvingly. "Thought I'd make a round of my nearby traps before chow and see if there were any fresh wapoose."

"What?"

"Rabbit," translated Dudley Shaw, opening the flap of a small packsack far enough to show me its furry white contents. "Have you eaten?"

"Yes, at the hotel. Dave Cuthill and Ted Boynton were telling me of some old cabins upriver. They said you'd know about them."

"I'm going to ramble up that way after breakfast," Dudley Shaw agreed. "How's the enemy?"

"Oh," I said after a moment. "It's almost eleven."

"Ghastly. Better stop in for some lap."

"Lap?"

"Tea," said Dudley Shaw. "Stimulating on a cold morning like this."

Warm winds and the sun had so lowered the snow along the river flat that, although after leaving Dudley Shaw's cabin we followed a snowshoe trail, neither of us wore webs. Often as a matter of fact, we found ourselves walking on hard bare ground.

There was just woods for something over half an hour; huge poplar, mostly, with tall spruce and slim lodgepole pine. Then the trail swung back toward the river's edge. Ahead in a clearing, log structures gleamed in the late Northern sunlight.

Dudley had detoured inland beside a small creek to examine some traps. My own pace quickened. With an almost choking sense of anticipation, I found myself waiting, the way you waited for anything that after an indeterminable time seemed suddenly close at hand, for my first full look at what might be our new home.

Through poplar trunks gnawed by moose I could make out rough roof shakes. Then log walls, rugged and substantial, widened into view. A lone window, as I approached it, successively reflected blue sky, then the white snow of the clearing, and finally the glitter of water rushing over the ice of a frozen brook.

Here was everything we needed, I thought: water, fuel, shelter, and beauty. The cabins stood near the edge of a brownish yellow cliff at whose foot, a hundred feet below, the river was a broad icy band pierced in two places by open water. A third log structure, inland of the other two, was partially hidden by high-bush cranberry and wild rose bushes, both reddish with edible berries.

Chinking, I could see now, had fallen out years before. Roofs were dilapidated. Yet most of the building materials seemed dry and sound. Windows were intact. One of the cabins, the newest of the trio, even retained a small cook stove that its former inhabitant, or Dudley Shaw perhaps, had greased so thoroughly that only where moisture had trickled down the capped pipe was there any corrosion.

There was even furniture. A chair built of hewn birch, painstakingly doweled and glued despite its roughness, was suspended from a ridgepole by wire, out of the reach of small animals which otherwise would have gnawed its moosehide seat and back.

"Government land," Dudley assured me upon his return. "A couple of trappers built that first cabin, then moved on. The last man to live up here was a gravel puncher."

"A prospector?"

"That's right. He made a dollar or two a day, sluicing for gold on a gravel bar below here. When the water got too low, he used a bucket at the end of a pole to move water into his box. Nights he joyously unhooked the bucket and made mulligan in it." Dudley chuckled. "Noble arrangement. Cheered him up vastly."

"Then Vena and I could settle here if we want?"

"Nobody to stop you," Dudley Shaw said. "If you ever got the notion, you could even buy what you wanted for five dollars an acre. Ghastly soil, though."

"We'd only want a small vegetable garden at most."

"The buildings are pretty well bogged down."

"There's plenty of seasoned wood. We wouldn't have to build with green logs and have them shrink for months." I stood looking around. "How's it up in the Canyon here for fish and game?"

"Noble," Dudley Shaw said. "Nobody rambles up this way but me."

"That's right, it is on your trapline."

"I was going to run this part of the line further inland anyway. Fisher are notorious for preferring the muskegs against the mountain. Glad to have some company at this end. We could have some cheery powwows."

Everything was so exactly what we had been dreaming about that I knew, even without her seeing it, that Vena couldn't help but find it perfect. Then I amended that. She couldn't, that is, if she liked the north woods at all.

4

Build It and It's Yours

Vena stood with me, watching Ted Boynton drive down the slit among the trees. The squeaking of dry snow beneath the runners disappeared first, then the creaking of wood and leather. Finally, dog, horses, and the sleigh with the round figure on its plank all vanished. The musical clangs of iron shoes became fewer and died away entirely.

A sense of aloneness gripped me. I found myself on an outjutting point, searching so I could point out the blur of the sleigh moving among trees. I even caught myself holding my breath, trying to capture some departing sound, which, the next instant, I told myself was foolish, because now didn't I have everything I had always wanted? Then I realized I was feeling this way in sympathy with Vena; because to her this must be more a violent twelve-month uprooting than a new life.

"Think of it as a camping trip," I said to Vena. But, somehow, I might still have been talking to myself, as I helped her move a kitchen cabinet to where we could begin packing some of the food in it.

"I'm afraid I haven't had much experience camping."

"Think of it as an overnight picnic, then," I said. "Here, let me."

I grabbed a box that she started to lift. Suddenly, I was overwhelmingly grateful to her for our being here, and I didn't want her to have to do anything that might keep her from liking it all.

"If you want some drinking water," I said, looking for the pails, "this in the brook is good. Dudley was telling me it comes from springs just behind us on Bullhead Mountain."

"I would like to wash out a few things before I put them away. And do we have a broom?"

"There's one around here somewhere." Then I felt guilty that she should be indoors worrying about a broom. "Before you do anything else, though, why don't you have a look around?"

"It's beautiful." She had always had the ability to lift her interest and mood far more facilely than I. "Are those moose tracks?"

"Yes," I said. Her hand curved through my arm, and I put my hand over hers. "The moose season is closed now. But we'll be able to get a bear when they come out of hibernation in a few weeks."

"Bear are good to eat?"

Bushman, who never got very far away, picked up his ears at the last word.

"I had some bear in New Brunswick last fall," I said, "and the roasts and stews taste even more like corn-fed beef than really prime deer and moose do. Their only drawback is that the meat is too coarse for good steaks. We ought to be able to get a glimpse of the waterfall from this point."

"I don't hear any waterfall."

"That's because it's frozen," I said. "What water there is still flowing just sort of trickles down the ice. We'd better not get too near the edge."

"Is there a way we can get down to the river?"

"Right over there." I showed her a gap in the cliffs, a

few yards upriver from where Bull Creek descended to the Peace in a glittering column. "It's gradual enough so that moose, as well as coyote and small animals, use it."

We stood looking at the great shaft of water-splattered ice awhile longer. But there were other things to see, and there was a lot to do before we would be ready for the early Northern night.

I'd taken care of some of these chores while Dudley Shaw had been elsewhere on his trapline, but now I had to finish patching the roof of the newest of the cabins while Vena handed up shakes I'd salvaged from one of the others. Then I emptied into a box the potatoes we'd just brought. The empty bag I took to a patch of swamp behind the clearing.

The snowfall lay sparsely there. It was possible without much effort to cram the sack with handfuls of sphagnum moss. This I wedged between the cabin logs wherever the clay chinking had dropped out. The walls bristled when I got through, but the building began to hold the heat from the small cook stove in which I'd started a quick fire after unwiring the lard-pail cap from its pipe.

"I suppose we'd better set up the heater we bought," I said. "The cook stove won't take anything but kindling. The airtight will take unsplit chunks, and it'll hold the fire overnight if we want."

"You look so serious," she smiled, and I found myself smiling, too.

"I guess I am," I said. "I want you to like it."

"Don't worry about me," she answered. Snow had gotten on her somehow, and there were drops of water on her hair and face. "I mean it, Brad. Please promise you won't worry about me."

"All right," I said. "I'll try not to."

"I don't want you ever worrying about my not being happy with the things that make you happy," she said. "Besides, there's no need."

Sunset our first day alone in the north woods was a magnificent thing, although it was strange to watch dusk lifting about the world in the middle of the afternoon. Bushman, head cocked, suddenly barked violently. He rushed to the edge of the cliff. Then he doubled back and began chasing himself in a great leaping circle. I heard the sound, too: a brief, sighing howl, like the yelp of a coyote only deeper and wilder.

I stood there, listening, in the deepening cold that came out of the darkness, hating to go indoors. Vena came and joined me. She had a streak of soot on her forehead, where she'd kept shoving shoulder-length hair back from her face, but she looked flushed and happy. When I laughed at her, she laughed back. Then she caught my hand.

"It's like being behind the scenes, isn't it?" she said.

"I never thought of it that way, but it is."

The frozen river had become a silver ornament, twining across the throat of the world. There was a feeling of newness, as of spring, in the air, although this may have been the result of the wind dying down. Most of all, it seemed perfectly natural for the two of us to be here. It was as if we were first arrivals, no longer automatons in an aimless chaos but, all at once, integral parts of an orderly cosmos.

That evening our coal oil lamp glowed, rather than shone, in a corner of the log cabin made snug by a hanging green tarpaulin. The soft light made our niche seem the cozier. Bushman was curled on a scrap of rug I'd found in one of the buildings, and at times he twitched as if still chasing rabbits. When I turned on the portable radio, Mexican and Californian stations boomed in without any of the man-made interference common in rural and city areas. Mostly, though, we talked.

That night we heard timber wolves. I had never supposed that any animals, particularly not in North America, could raise such a din: like that of two trains unexpectedly screaming past one another at a dark grade crossing. Stepping around Bushman, who kept close to me, I shuffled toward the frosted luminosity of a window. I felt Vena's warmth beside me, as my palm cleared a pane. Together we watched shadowy forms moving in a single line up the icy road of river. They blurred out of sight at last against the crouching shapes of bluffs.

After that, I couldn't get to sleep for a long time. Rather than feeling any sense of oppression, though, I was caught up in an expanding excitement that seemed too exquisite to lose in sleep. Although the night was cold on my face, I was warm inside the eiderdown sleeping robe. As always, the partially inflated air mattress, even though it was only spread on rough flooring, seemed more comfortable than the most expensive conventional mattress on which I'd ever lain. I remembered this was Vena's first experience with one.

"Is it soft enough?" I asked her. "I didn't get it blown up too hard?"

There was no reply except for the thump of Bushman's tail. I became aware of Vena's slow, regular breathing. I heard other things, too, in the northern silence that was not stillness at all but a great peace— wind, swaying trees, water, shifting ice, two hunting owls, the song of some smaller bird like frozen moonlight tinkling, distant coyote, and the nearby scamper of what sounded like a flying squirrel.

Our eventual cabin like this one, I realized, should not shut out nature but should merely be a shelter in the midst of nature. Drowsily, I began picturing the sort of log home that would satisfy us both.

I started to work the next day salvaging building materials. My tools were our ax, saw, chisel, and hammer, along with a wrecking bar and a small block and tackle borrowed from Ted Boynton. The clay chinking, plus insulative layers of loam in the roofs, made the job a dusty one.

The two of us tried to visualize the exact best spot for a cabin. I wanted to be in the open where, when spring arrived, the winds that always blow along a river would keep mosquitoes away. Vena, on the other hand, didn't want to get too near the edge of the cliff. Ted Boynton had privately agreed with me, pointing out that a great many people made the mistake of building too far back in the bush, although Vena had no thought of going to that extreme. Then Dudley, who stopped by for lunch, told Vena she was right about not wanting to build on the edge, although I never meant that, either.

Things went better after I'd sharpened four stakes and joined them with strings of the proper lengths. Vena moved them into different positions, while Bushman romped about her and snatched up mouthfuls of snow. I'd see her pressing the stakes into the crusted snow of the clearing, then going inside the cabin-size rectangle to pretend she was working at the stove or reading at the windows. Finally, she was satisfied, and I found I was satisfied, too.

We decided to build our wilderness home near the riverside, in the angle between brook and the trail down to the Peace. We measured, counted, and drew plans before determining that the most advantageous way we could make use of the materials at hand was by erecting a cabin twenty feet long and twelve feet wide. Four double windows should be banked on the long south side that paralleled the Peace River.

Once the site was decided upon, Vena helped all she could with the lighter work. Boards were stacked by lengths at one side. Slabs went into other orderly piles, not because I, at least, was especially orderly, but because it would save time that way. The various items of salvagable hardware were tossed into separate boxes.

I remember the spicy odor that clung to the logs, the freshness of the breezes that kept moving downriver, and the rushing of open water in brook and river. I remember how the sun, that gave a flat sheen to the ice, caught the leaping rivulets and brought them alive. Once we were caught up in the enterprise, we found we couldn't let it go. We had put off exploring the countryside until we should be snugly housed. Now the icy highways beckoned more and more urgently, speeding our efforts.

There's something about building a home of your own that reaches deep within one, touching almost forgotten ancestral memories and bringing all of you alert. Vena felt it, too, I know, perhaps even more than I did because, intrinsically, a home means more to a woman. She was always the first to want to start again each morning. This enthusiasm on our parts, I suppose, made up for a lot of technical shortcomings, although there aren't many ways you can go wrong when building a log cabin.

The weather continued blue and bright. Nights, while I lay briefly awake and went over the morrow's already carefully drawn and detailed steps, an occasional raucous gust sometimes gave a new turn to my thoughts. But we always awoke to a wind still blowing warm and fair out of the west. The breezes quieted at dawn, as they did again at dusk. But once the work was underway again, they were already romping anew, sometimes rolling particles of snow that Bushman chased, barking, across the flat.

The eighth day after the construction had been started I finished the roof and the floor, while Vena filled the seams between the wall logs with smooth bands of wet clay. She finally held the door, carefully spaced with chips, while I screwed the hinges into place. Then we stood inside and savored the results of our joint efforts.

"I hope all this isn't going to be too crowded for you," I said.

"After theatre dressing rooms and after living out of a suitcase in hotels?" She threw an arm around me.

"No, this is wonderful: to have a home all our own. I'm just trying to get everything straight in my mind. Now, if we put a stand over there with some shelves under it—."

"Look," I said, "we've a box we can use for now. Why don't you begin bringing over the things we'll need right away, while I'm setting up the stoves?"

"What things?"

"The dishes, food, and such," I said. Then I laughed at her puzzled look. "We have our shelter now. Let's not waste any more of this good weather."

We could follow the Peace River into the mountains. There would be enough stormy days later when, confined in any event, we could work on the cabin's interior.

"All right," she said. "What shall I wear?"

I know now that all this glaring white immensity still frightened her, but I didn't realize it then. No doubt the possibility of becoming lost was foremost in her mind.

"Get on your ski clothes if you want. Just don't wear anything too heavy."

"All right," she agreed. Then she wanted to know if we should eat first.

"Why don't I pack a lunch?" I said.

I wanted us to discover what lay beyond the narrowing canyon into whose slit, about a mile by shoreline above the cabin, the river disappeared. I could already see us stopping somewhere in a sunny niche, where perhaps no other human had ever set foot, and piling up driftwood for a fire.

5

Sidewalk in the Wilderness

Snow, although not more than a foot deep in the wilderness behind our cabin, was too dense and granular for comfortable walking. Along the edge of the Peace River, however, stretched an icy sidewalk that was smoother and more inviting than any concrete strip I'd trod in any city.

"It's marvelous," Vena said.

Then she slipped. I caught her. Then my feet almost went out from under me, and we both began laughing.

"You do have to be careful, though. It's a lot like life, isn't it?" She clasped my arm with both of hers, and she rested her head on my shoulder. "Everything seems to be going along smoothly, and then you take a jolt. When everything begins moving too smoothly, I guess that's the time to watch out."

"I suppose so, although I like it smooth."

"You are happy here, aren't you, Brad?"

"Yes, I'm happy if you are."

"I guess that's why I'm so happy, too." She moved her head so that she could look at me. "I'm afraid I'm not very good at this sort of thing, but I'll do my best."

"Why, you're doing wonderfully."

"I want to do my best, to make it the most memorable year you—we ever had."

The icy sidewalk wound on and on up the river.

There were occasional rough places, and in one spot an upthrusting reef made a rocky barrier over which we had to scramble. Now and then an inch or two of water caught at our feet, giving our rubber soles traction.

"It's marvelous," Vena said again, and I found myself liking the porcelainlike glow the white winter gleam gave her face. "Whatever makes it this way?"

It took me a moment to realize she was talking about the slickness underfoot, and I tried to explain it the way it had been told to me: how the river never completely froze. When temperatures fell, channels clogged with running ice, forcing water out as overflow. Then there was the water that spread over the ice when warm west winds melted the snow, and there was the water from brooks and springs. All this sought the lowest levels, and where the river was consistently lower was along the shores.

The ribbony flatness extended in other directions, too, following valleys among hummocks and ridges and jumbles of ice and forming beckoning mazes. Bushman investigated some of these, but for once he was having a slow time of it. His claws kept rasping, and his efforts to maintain footing kept him continually off balance. When he bounded over the rough surface he wasn't much better off, for then he had to watch out for hollow crust and deep cracks.

"Here, Bush," I called one time when he loped close to an open stretch of rushing water.

It was about two hundred yards across the Peace at that particular point, and the yellowish brown cliffs on the other side echoed my voice. Bushman had started in our direction. Now he stopped, head cocked, and turned back. When he did romp to us, we yelled again, and the echo took him to the opposite shore, frisking and barking.

A raw north wind had started blowing about the cabin before we'd left, but down here on the river just enough breeze stirred to bend the heat waves that lifted lazily from ice, snow, and water. Sunlight reflected at us from every angle. I soon unbuttoned one of my woolen shirts and then the other. Eventually, I removed both and buckled them to my packsack. The air felt good on my skin.

Vena motioned about her. "I don't believe it."

"I hardly believe it myself."

"They'll certainly never believe us back in Boston," she said, and then she laughed with sheer exuberance.

Another of the things those who knew her wouldn't have readily credited back in the city, I thought, was how well she looked in ski clothes and leather-topped boots. When I told Vena this, she laughed again, only differently.

"That's because I'm happy," she said. "Everybody looks good when they're happy, and I'm far happier than I have a right to be."

"Right?" I said. "How do you mean?"

"Because I never expected to be, not here," she said. "It still scares me, the vastness of everything and not being able to make much of an impression on it. But I'm beginning to like it a lot."

A cool breeze came out of the shadows of the narrow gap in the river bed which Dudley Shaw had told us was called Box Canyon, although of course it wasn't really that unless you thought of it as a box with both ends open. Even as I buttoned my shirts back on, I was thinking how glad I was to be here. There was the excitement of exploring new unspoiled places. The undercurrent of unharnessed vigor, like the water always rushing beneath the ice, gave a feeling of great vitality to everything.

"Aren't you getting hungry?" Vena asked. "Doesn't all this make you feel alive and hungry?"

"There ought to be a place up ahead," I said. It was to be our first trail meal, and I wanted everything to be as ideal as possible for her.

Bushman was sniffing at the tracks of the wolves we'd seen the first night. They led in a single line through the deeper snow of the Canyon, where each animal had followed in the footsteps of the leader. When Bushman finished his examination, I was glad his instincts caused him to follow us more closely. It was a trick of wolves, we'd heard, for one of them to lure a lone dog into the bush where the pack would be waiting to finish him, and I hoped Bush would never lose his instinctive caution.

"Smart boy," I said, and I patted his head. Then I saw, where a high bench along the north shore shelved down to the river, a bright jumble of boulders. "How's about making our fire up there?"

The point was almost a mile away. When we reached it, I saw it hid a widening curve of river set with several islands. My spine tingled, for just ahead, friendly under glittering snow, was the broad bulk of Bullhead Mountain.

"Tell me what I can do," Vena was saying.

"Why," I said, "you just take it easy. You must be tired. I'll get everything started."

I found where large rocks made a semicircle. This I cleared of snow with a few swipes of my feet. There was a huge block of clay ironstone, in front of which I could kindle the fire, which would act as a sort of chimney whose partial vacuum would keep the smoke out of our faces.

Wood was plentiful: dry softwood which had been stranded by high water and, on the shore, seasoned poplar. While I was getting an armful of the latter, it took only a moment to strip enough green boughs from a spruce to floor one end of the niche.

When I asked Vena if she'd like to light the campfire, she seemed pleased.

"It's going," she said finally, and she sounded surprised, although she had gone about it efficiently as she did with everything, protecting the match flame from drafts with her body.

"Sure, it's going," I said. "Everything you do goes fine."

"Does it?" she said. "Sometimes I feel as useless as a hothouse flower."

"Why, you're not like that at all," I said. "Besides, hothouse flowers have lots of uses."

"Not in the North," she said.

I'd made a tea pail before leaving the cabin by punching two nail holes in the opposite sides of a large fruit juice can, just below the rim, and looping a wire between them. This, filled with icicles and suspended over the blaze, began to darken in the heat. Smoke from birch bark and spruce gave the topmost ice a black coating that never remained constant, for the ice was already melting.

Bushman was staying nearby, now that I had taken the lunch out of my packsack. I sharpened two green sticks. After charring them, I strung them with small, salted squares of the moose meat Ted Boynton had given us. I thrust the kabobs briefly into the flame to seal in the juices.

"Do you mind holding these?" I asked Vena. "Just keep them in the fringes of the heat, turning them a little so that they'll roast all over. I'll be getting the bannock ready."

"That's bread, isn't it? But you didn't bring a pan, did you?"

"Suppose we had to survive after an atomic bomb," I asked, "and there wasn't a pan?"

"Suppose there wasn't any flour, either?"

"Then we could powder the inner bark of those birch trees or those poplars. But there is flour; also baking powder, shortening, and salt. That's what I was mixing back at the cabin. Now, I'll just borrow a bit of this ice water. We'll make a dough. And we'll wind it on this stick."

The way she laughed was as if she was laughing at herself.

"I might have known you'd have the answer."

"Wait until you taste it, Vena. If it works out, maybe it'll be something you'll like to make yourself later on. Pretty soon you're going to be doing all the cooking."

I thought she might object, but what she said was, "I'd like to try. I don't like being just an ornament."

"Why, you never could be just that."

There seemed to be an empty whistle in the free, wild sound of the wind, as it surged around the point. I thought it might just seem that way because of the nearby cheerful crackling of the fire, but occasional gusts that swooped across our faces carried the smell of snow.

The sky was still a bright, clear blue. Clouds that moved puffily across it were dazzling white. Meat sputtered. The ribbon of bread swelled and browned.

"Come and get it," I said, and I added, "or I'll throw it away."

Bushman began barking.

The moose meat, juicy and rare beneath its salt-glazed char, was delicious. We nibbled it directly from our individual spits and broke off steaming chunks of hot campfire bread and spread them liberally with dripping butter. Strong black tea, in stainless steel cups that were cool to the lips, set off the unforgettable flavors.

Vena had been gazing into the embers, while Bushman, who'd gulped down his own meal, was nosing around for any dropped tidbits. Now she looked at me.

"I'd like to plant a little garden in the spring, Brad."

"Good," I said, "that'll be our vegetables. It'll be work, though. If you'd rather, we can get most of our vegetables from the woods themselves."

"That will be fun, too, of course," she said slowly.

"But ever since I talked to Mrs. Ferguson at the hotel, I've been thinking of a little garden all my own: things like carrots, beets, parsley, onions, cabbages, and radishes. Then I'll be doing something to help."

"Why," I said, "that will be wonderful."

Sparks soared when I shoved the end of a limb into the fire. Then flame started to curl around the dry wood, sending up pinkish prongs through which I could see the sparkle of a frozen 300-foot waterfall on the opposite shore. More and more, now that we'd feasted, the accumulated fatigue of building our cabin seemed to cushion me down.

I must have dozed off. Vena did, certainly, because the next thing I knew the fire was almost out. A cold wind, laced with snow, was prodding the shoreline. All that remained of the sun was a bright streak high among the southwestern spruce. The river ice was booming with frost.

"Wake up," I urged Vena, while Bushman stretched and wagged an encouraging tail. "It's time to get started back. Are you awake, Vena?"

It was storming hard before we were halfway home. Snow drove into our eyes. It also hid the ice and made progress a sliding, skidding affair.

"Keep hold of this," I told her, handing her a long driftwood pole and looking for another one for myself. "In case we should go through, it'll bridge the crack."

"All right."

Gale wind whipped at us along the river canyon that, perhaps originally a crack in the earth's surface, had been sculptured through the entire backbone of the Canadian Rockies by centuries of scouring air and water. A fresh flurry of snow began funneling through the chasm with suffocating whiteness.

"Is Bushman there?" I asked.

"Yes, he keeps bumping into my heels. Is it a blizzard?"

"No," I said, "they don't have them here in the

mountains. It's just the wind along the river with nothing to stop it."

The cabin became a welcome bulge in the snow-heaving whiteness. The whittled latch moved clumsily in my mittened fingers. The hinges squealed. There was the hollow clatter of the door when a gust pulled it out of my grasp.

Flakes eddied after us into the single room. When I leaned my weight against the door long enough to let the latch rattle back into its catch, the still cold seemed more penetrating than the surging frigidity outdoors.

Wind, fresh from the Arctic Circle eleven degrees farther North, pressed the sweet oily blackness of birch smoke back down the stovepipe. I fed the crackling white bark with split spruce and banged on the lids. The kindling caught with a heady snapping and popping.

While the fire was building its ardent rumble, I replenished our water and wood supply so I wouldn't have to go out for either for awhile after we had changed our clothes. Then we brushed off Bushman as well as we could with a stiff broom. He concluded the job with a happy shake that started at his head and ended with a great flourish of grey tail.

Vena and I got on dry clothes. Then we stood at the window nearest the stove. It felt good to know that all three of us were safely indoors while snow stroked roof, walls, and glass. The flakes seemed to be falling lazily now. Although snow, like an enormous banner, unfurled out of Box Canyon in wind that howled in a twisting rush along the river bed, here on the high cut bank it all seemed a million light years away.

Here in our cabin we had everything we needed and, for once uncluttered, we needed everything we had, including one another. I realized I had never felt snugger, or safer, or happier.

"Contented?" I asked Vena.

"Very contented," she said.

6

Two Inches Below Zero

Flakes continued to waft downward the next few days, as they sometimes do on a high barometer in the North, never falling fast but always inching higher. It didn't seem to make any difference in any event, now that the back of winter was broken and the days were becoming perceptibly longer. Besides, Vena and I were indoors most of the time, building furniture and making the interior of the cabin comfortable. It was pleasant to be working together in such agreeable intimacy, with no need to run down to the corner store and no reason, either, to watch the clock.

The cold, when it arrived, swooped upon us. The day was approaching the dusky blueness of late afternoon when I particularly liked to be outdoors. Vena had earlier walked down the trail to Dudley Shaw's to get the mail, which he's been kind enough to pick up at the post office. Now she was occupied with the leisurely preparations for supper.

I was sawing some lengths of dry poplar, and carrying them across our brook to where I could conveniently split them later, when I realized that a north wind was cutting under the warm westerly. The next time I took a chunk of wood under each arm to the side of the cabin, I looked at the thermometer. The red line of alcohol stood just above zero.

Feathery flakes had been skittering downward. Now, hard sharp pellets were beginning to sting my face. On the next trip, perhaps five minutes later, I met Vena on her way back from the cache.

"Look at that," she said. "Seven below zero. When do you want me to put in the macaroni and cheese?"

"Oh, any time you say. I'm almost finished with the wood. Do you mind setting out the water buckets, please?"

The temperature was down another four degrees by the time I came to pick up the buckets. The water hole had frozen, but I could hear the stream gurgling beneath. A few bangs with the back of the ax broke away the shell of ice. The rush of water, when I dipped in the first pail, almost tore the handle out of my hand. Water surged over my fingers. Back in the cabin, it felt good to warm my hands.

"Did you remember the kindling for tomorrow morning?" Vena asked, putting up the wings on the table.

"It's in the oven," I said. "Unless there's something else you want from the cache, I'm done outside except for bringing in a few more logs. It might be a good idea to keep the heater going tonight."

Vena was lighting the coal oil lamp. The wick wreathed with flame, and while she bent to adjust it, lights and shadows played across her face. A soft radiance agreeably filled the room.

"So that's what is in the oven?" She smiled, and all of a sudden I sensed a rich, warm glow at just being here, with the cold sweeping in, and about to sit down to a supper we were both hungry enough to enjoy. "I couldn't see what was giving me so much trouble when I was putting in Bushman's food."

"Is that what smells so good?" I asked.

Just outside the windows Bushman began barking,

perhaps because he had heard his name, or because it was near his mealtime, or possibly because he also caught the smell.

"Everything always gets in the oven," Vena said. "Now I suppose it's time to put in the Indian pudding, if you don't mind stirring up that ice cream for it."

She opened the oven door, and there was the spicy odor of warm pine mingling with the cereal-like aroma of dog meal. The combination set my taste buds tingling.

"I don't mind," I said. "When do we eat?"

"I thought you weren't in any hurry. Oh, I suppose half an hour should do it." When she reached past me for the pot holders, she gave me a hug. "Poor Bushman. Now he'll have to wait for his pan to cool."

Bushman, who was resting his forefeet on the window sill, sounded sorry for himself. His gaze shifted to Vena, who was pouring a can of evaporated milk into a large bowl and adding sugar and vanilla extract, and his tail wagged. She gave the bowl to me, along with a big spoon. When I stepped outside to stir in clean snow from the top of a woodpile, the temperature stood at fifteen degrees below zero.

It had dropped another six degrees by bedtime. The Aurora Borealis hung like an immense drapery below the North Star. Its fold shimmered and scintillated with ethereal electricity. We stood on the doorstep and watched it until cold, penetrating our shell of warmth, sent us inside, Bushman a scurrying grey wraith between us.

The windows were frosted when I stirred comfortably in my eiderdown the next morning. Hunching up on one elbow, with a cold draft funneling down my back, I finally located a clear streak along the top of one pane.

Moonlight showed a luminous ceiling of frost that stretched slightly above the stovepipe height across the platinum whiteness of the frozen landscape. It had

stopped snowing. For a moment I wondered if the two
open stretches in the river had somehow drifted over.
Then I could make out that the air above them was
white with fog.

"Do you want to go out, Bush?" I whispered, and as
usual I clumped sleepily out of bed to open the door
for him.

This morning, though, he prodded the outside air
with a doubtful nose, then tried to double back into the
cabin. I gave him a push. While I was standing there, I
glanced at the thermometer. Then I went back for my
flashlight. I finally found the colored alcohol. It was
barely protruding above its glass bulb.

"Is it cold?" Vena asked drowsily.

I closed the door carefully.

"Fifty degrees below zero," I said.

"Oh," she said, "fifty—. Fifty below zero!"

"See for yourself."

There was the sound of the eiderdown unsnapping,
the thump of bare feet, and then the shuffle of fur-lined
moccasins. She moved quickly beside me, pulling a
Christmas-red robe over a blue nylon nightgown more
appropriate for hotel living. The straight lines of the
flannel gave her a slim, childlike appearance that
seemed more in keeping when her fists pounded my
chest with pretended exasperation.

"Well," Vena said, "aren't you going to open the
door and let me see?"

When I did open the door, Bushman bounded in
with so much bouncy enthusiasm that she started
laughing.

"Why, it really is fifty below." She had a second
look, then a long gaze about the clearing, before she
scampered, shivering, for the heater. "Brad, isn't it exciting? Why, darling, you seem serious all of a sudden."

"I was just thinking that I'm pretty lucky," I said,

opening the flue of the airtight and starting to drop wood atop the still bright coals. "Weather like this could be pretty miserable if you let it be. So could a lot of things up here. And if you thought that way, you'd soon start feeling miserable yourself."

"But I don't," she said. "I'm not."

"I know, but if you did, I'd begin feeling badly, too. Either that, or I'd find myself building a defensive wall against your moods. I suppose that's what happens in a lot of marriages. The paths part, and a wall gets between."

Particles of heavying frost, similar to great snow-flakes but more fragile, were drifting downward in the still air.

"It is exciting, though, isn't it?" Vena was saying, and I caught the lift in her voice.

"What?"

"The cold? You must sense it, too." She looked around swiftly, drawing her robe prettily around her. Her eyes were bright. "I never thought it would be anything like this."

Neither had I although, now that I thought about it, what was cold but the opposite of heat? So why shouldn't a really cold morning have the opposite effect of what is often described as a warm, lazy afternoon? I'd heard before that an undercurrent of excitement characterizes all extreme cold in the Far North, and now I could believe that.

There was a peace to it, too, I realized, and a great, stirring exhilaration that gripped you even when you were warm and comfortable and indoors. The feeling carried with it an exaltation that I'd never even come close to perceiving in the artificial disorder of any city.

For a moment I wondered if the sensation could be a reaction to the danger that lay like an abyss in the frozen immensity about the cabin, waiting to trap the unwary. Then I decided it couldn't be that, for although you could die if you gave way to such temperatures, you could perish just as readily if far more unpleasantly in the opposite extremes in which I'd occasionally sweltered in the desert.

Besides, no very immediate danger confronted Vena and me. We needed warmth if we were to stay alive, certainly. But if our fires for some reason gave out, there was always the life-insuring snugness of our eiderdowns. The feeling, I concluded, must arrive from an atavistic comprehension of the primeval nothingness of all this. For just as heat is energy, so is cold a lack of energy. Cold is nothing, just as before the heat of creation there was nothingness.

"Aren't you awake yet?" Vena was saying with a sudden lifting of her head. "You never thought cold would be anything like this, did you?"

"No," I said, looking at her. "I didn't dare hope you'd be like this, either. I'm satisfied all around."

The sun, when it finally rolled into view, was a lopsided red disk that wheeled misshapenly above the blanched horizon. We ate, looking at how the sun's rays gleamed off the snow and made the inside of the cabin brightly white.

"It's like that poem by John Greenleaf Whittier we studied soon after starting school," Vena said. " 'No cloud above, no earth below—A universe of sky and snow'."

But although there were none of the usual cumulus clouds scouring the heavens, a gleaming layer of condensed moisture spread like a gossamer canopy over the throbbing ground a few feet above cabin height.

Frost was accumulating, too, in a feathery sheathing on every exposed surface. Trunk, branches, and twigs of a birch just outside the windows no longer formed a wintry skeleton. They now shimmered, in a fairy-book design, with a sort of chinchilla furriness that, in the sunlight, seemed intricately spun of fiberized gems. The coating on the top branches was transparent against the chill blue sky.

One doesn't often sense awe in this day and age, but I felt it now.

"Isn't it incredible?" Vena's words were almost a whisper. "I've seen something of the sort just outside Paris, but never so stark and simple."

"Sometimes on the Esplanade in Boston, right after a storm," I said, "you'll find the snow and mist crystallized on the trees like carved ivory. But it's never delicate like this."

"The air is so still. I suppose that's one reason." She looked at me all of a sudden. "What's that banging noise?"

"The ice is freezing more solidly, and it's expanding and cracking. So is the ground, for that matter."

"I know those sounds. They're like cannon. The sounds I mean are more like rifles."

"I guess that's the sap freezing and splitting the trees."

It was misty over the river where the two open gaps of rushing water steamed upon contact with air that was now some 80° colder.

No life seemed to be moving outdoors. Then Bushman began growling and wanting to get out. There was the swish of snowbirds, like alabaster sparrows, sweeping through a band of sunlight and landing to peck at his food pan. When I opened the frost-rimmed door at his scratching insistence, inrolling cold marked its heavy presence with a white fog that advanced in billows across the floor.

Bushman soon wanted in again, appearing at the windows in white-whiskered concern and holding up first one foot and then another. The icicled appearance of his muzzle made us laugh. But when we went out, moisture from Vena's breath quickly sketched silvery crescents along her eyebrows and heavied strands of hair that fell across her forehead.

"What are you laughing at?" I asked.

"I'm glad I don't have whiskers," she said. "Yours are all white around your mouth."

"Bushman and I," I said.

Although frost gave a soft luminosity to this strangely glistening white world, there was a clarity to everything that was perhaps largely the result of sharpened perceptions. Spring intoxicates, I thought. Summer relaxes. Autumn arouses, while winter sharpens the senses. The air was as stimulating as a dozen cups of coffee.

I didn't feel the cold at first. Then it was suddenly like stepping over the tops of waders. Everything was warm, and then abruptly my entire body seemed saturated with coldness. Our arms filled with firewood, we shoved back indoors. There the moderate heat seemed, by contrast, all the more wonderful. Bushman, who'd quickly snaked in ahead of us, was luxuriating in it, too, his tail wagging ingratiatingly.

"Well, here's the weather we've been waiting for," Vena said.

"Waiting for?" I asked.

"You didn't want us to work indoors while the weather was so nice. Well, now's our chance to finish getting everything inside shipshape."

7

Sun Dogs

Shelves, we were to find, assume an exaggerated importance in log cabin living. We put them wherever we could locate the space. None ever appeared out of place, and there never seemed to be enough of them.

As a matter of fact, as Vena noted—particularly in reference to my own corner which quickly assumed an orderly confusion, although not to me, of books and papers and personal belongings—the only trouble was that most of the shelves soon became so crowded that they seemed cluttered. She solved this to some extent by curtaining those she could, choosing a red material that blended brightly with the logs and the wilderness.

It can be seen that such a simple object as a wooden box could become, in the woods, an object of great treasure. With its reinforced back nailed to the wall, it afforded at the very least a spacious top ledge and, below, a compartment that Vena could either drape or edge congruously with red trimming. Even that first morning, the cabin became more and more like home.

"How do you happen to be so handy at this sort of thing?" I asked her.

"You should see some of the theatre dressing rooms I've had to make do with."

The furniture was simplicity itself. We'd brought

from town a heavy kitchen cabinet, with drawers and a bin, and a wing table that occupied a satisfactorily small space when closed. Besides counters for preparing meals, we needed only one additional table, for my typewriter, and two straight chairs with their seats a functional foot below the table tops.

When we wanted extra chairs, all we had to do was bring in chunks of log sawed for the heater but left unsplit. These proved so convenient, in fact, that Vena covered one to make a barrel-like hassock. An easy chair was already on the premises, which was sufficient as Vena came to prefer to read on her bunk with pine-needle pillows between her and the wall to give a chaise-longue effect.

The cold continued that day. For awhile toward noon sunlight glinting on the thermometer lifted the column of alcohol to 30° below zero and gave an illusion of warmth.

"Why alcohol?" Vena asked. "I thought good thermometers used mercury."

"Not in the North. Mercury freezes at 38° below zero. Grain alcohol stays liquid for something like 141° colder. Matter of fact, Dudley was telling me that's one way sourdoughs hereabouts tell how potent their liquor is by the amount of ice crystals in the bottle in really cold weather."

Once evening approached, we lost part of ourselves in books. I was away with D'Artagnan, Athos, Porthos, and Aramis. Vena was reading the essays of the man who said: "Cast out fear; rely on your own inner resources; trust life and it will repay your trust. You can do better than you believe you can."—Ralph Waldo Emerson.

The night seemed a small thing at first, closed in by shores of mist. Even with the company of an overnight fire crackling companionably in the airtight heater, I found myself looking forward to the spaciousness of morning.

It was Vena who first noticed the Northern Lights. The long rays we saw first were like the bars of a silvery gate. Then these bars widened and lengthened, as if the gate were opening toward us. Suddenly, we could see beyond into what might have been a celestial garden.

"Look at that color, Brad."

Green was predominant, the sort of bright light verdancy that's prevalent in springtime. There were the reds and yellows and pinks of flowers, too. These started as buds. Some unfurled like bursting poppies. Others became long gladioli, with huge transparent petals almost hiding their single-bladed leaves. Then it was as if entire beds flowered in individual masses of radiance. The garden deepened, obscuring more and more of the artfully placed ground lights that were in reality stars.

The next morning we awoke to a blanched world. Moonlight, shining on frost and snow, gave enough light so we did not bother with the lamps at first. I'd been apprehensive lest the long winter months be dark and depressing. But the fact was that the extreme dryness and clearness of atmosphere, plus the reflective qualities of the whitened wilderness, greatly magnified even the brightness of the stars. These filled the sky like glistening pebbles at the seashore, the surf being the now palely rippling Aurora Borealis.

"Want to go out, Bush?" I asked.

Bushman, usually eager to start each new day, made believe he didn't hear.

"Has it warmed up any?" came a voice.

All I could see was a shadowy countenance almost hidden beneath the upper folds of the eiderdown.

"I'll look," I said. "I've got to get a couple more logs for the heater, anyway."

The beam of the flashlight showed the temperature was down to 55° below zero. The falling frost had left a fresh surface, but the only tracks I could find about the cabin were several little runways of the ever-busy field mice. I tried to locate two logs that had branch stubs on them so I could carry one in each hand. The light of my flash died out. I rattled and jarred it several times before I realized what had happened. The batteries, already cold from having been on a window sill all night, had frozen.

It gave me an eerie feeling. About that time the coldness bit into me, too. I slammed back indoors. It wasn't that I meant to slam. But even the wood in the door had shrunk with cold, and the door fitted its frame with unexpected looseness.

Vena must have thought I'd done it on purpose. Or else the noise startled her, too. I heard her muffled tones, "I was just getting up."

"It's early yet. Why not let the cabin get warm? How about coffee in bed for a change?"

"You've talked me into it," she said.

But after one steaming cup, she was also out of bed. Neither of us was finding these Northern days long enough, although remembering many a late morning's slumber being troubled by the nervous clatter of the big city, I couldn't recall ever having had that difficulty in Boston. Too, the early mornings here were such pleasures, partly because of the quality they had of freeing one of trivial concerns and somehow spurring the enthusiasms to soar, that we found ourselves willing even to steal a few hours from the night to lengthen them.

"Why are you staring off into space?" Vena asked, stopping beside me.

"I was just thinking." She looked slim and pretty in slacks and sweater. "Why, is there anything you'd like to have me do? Are you warm enough?"

"Oh, yes," she said.

One advantage of the small cabin, we were discovering, is that heat takes a comparatively brief time to fill it with agreeable warmth. Even on such a morning, when the seasoned logs were contracting and when every wall nail was dotted with frost, it was cozy indoors.

Firewood snapped, while outside the ice cannonaded, the ground cracked noisily, and trees snapped with the intensity of detonating cartridges. The temperature diminished to 63° below zero during the day.

When we went out to see what weather nearly 100° below freezing felt like, our breaths froze about us with a crackling noise that reminded me of crisp paper being crumpled. Vena, however, perhaps because her ears were warmly muffled with her longish brown hair, said that the sound seemed more to her like swishing silk.

The stovepipe was spraying forth white smoke that flattened against the ghostly radiance of the frost ceiling. The day did not feel unusually bitter for the first few minutes. Then frigidity gripped with astounding speed, even though I'd brought out the warmed ax and was energetically splitting some wood which Vena was gathering and taking indoors.

My face was affected most. I kept feeling my nose and other exposed portions to make sure they did not become numb and hard, and I saw to it that Vena did the same thing. Once, when my stiffening forehead lost feeling, I bared a hand long enough to cup a warm palm over the frostbitten part which was soon warm and tingling again. I rewarmed the hand by shoving it inside my shirt. I was still holding it there when Vena reappeared outdoors, this time with two water pails.

"Will we have to melt ice for water?" she asked.

"I don't think so," I said. "Did you bring something we can ladle with?"

"The small saucepan is right inside."

The brook, its channels clogging with ice, was overflowing and freezing in a slowly broadening pattern. Testing the fresh ice with the ax, I found just below the surface along the nearer shore several inches of water.

Some of this spattered as I dipped. When fresh water hit the bare ice, nothing happened. But when the drippings began to contact newly frozen spatterings, these latter melted just enough so that, refreezing, the whole gave off a crackling sound like that of an exploding pack of firecrackers.

"I wonder," I said.

"What do you wonder?"

"You've probably read some of those stories about men spitting in real cold weather, fifty below or so, and the saliva freezing between their lips and the ground. Unless someone happened to be standing on a cliff, obviously saliva couldn't very well chill from body temperature to freezing in the instant it would take to fall. But if it should happen to hit on some newly frozen moisture, it would cause a snapping sound that might give that impression."

"Oh?" she said.

The slush present in the brook's flowing water was floating to the top of the buckets, dulling the surface.

"Here, I'll take one pail," Vena volunteered. "It'll be easier."

The snow beneath our feet bunched and rasped like gravel. When I brushed against some frozen green willows, the branches snapped off like icicles. My nasal passages became clogged, as if with ice, and I had to breathe through my mouth, shoving a mittened palm over it to keep the cold air from causing a burning sensation in my lungs.

"Bushman wants to go in," Vena was shivering.

"I don't think he's the only one."

The wolfhound scrambled ahead of us as we opened the door. My jarred bucket slopped. I watched the water become an opaque white ridge on the floor while Vena was going for a mop.

The inrolling mist of the encroaching cold did not disappear for moments after we'd latched the door.

Slowly we became warm again. The color of the single room, as well as its heat, seemed all the more pleasant because of its contrast to the whitened wilderness outside.

That day, for some reason, I could not sit still and read when our work was done. I found myself pacing, not so much uneasily as with an overflowing of energy. I set myself to putting a real edge on my knives in anticipation of the time, not far away, when bear would be coming out of hibernation. It took only a pleasant half-hour more to sharpen my fishhooks for the days when rainbow trout, Dolly Varden, ling, and Arctic grayling would be ravenous in the river below.

Vena, I noticed, occupied herself with better arranging her belongings, in tidying the kitchen shelves, and then in a bout of cleaning. It was a restless and yet restful day, shrouded in the cotton batten of the frost haze.

"It's spectacular," Vena said one time. "But is that because we can sit on the sidelines and watch everything? How about the trappers and the lumberjacks and such who have to work in such weather?"

"They're on the sidelines, too. That's one reason why extreme cold isn't too much of a problem to the sourdough. He just sits it out. Do you know what causes most of the accidental deaths in the Far North?"

"No."

"It's just the opposite of cold," I said. "It's fire."

The sky, its blue softened by the haze which rested like a white light over the earth, seemed that afternoon to take on the translucence of fine china. Then it was as if the sun's heat above and the earth's cold below were suddenly too violent a strain. The heavens seemed to explode into a trillion glowing particles.

"What," Vena said, grasping my arm, "what is it?"

"Ice crystals floating across the sun."

Like everyone else, I'd seen basically the same phenomenon before, when rays gleaming through the same

innumerable spangles of moisture—frozen because no
water can remain liquid in the intense frigidity of such
heights, far above when the rain clouds and the thun-
derheads form—made the ring around the sun and the
even more familiar halo about the moon. But both
these spectacles were like still pictures, whereas now
the innumerable glinting ice crystals were seething in
the tumultuous upper atmosphere.

"Look, Vena."

The swollen sun itself, magnified by the countless
frozen particles, seemed to burst and to cascade earth-
ward in a confusion of fire. Through its skeletal
remains, a golden beam expanded, parallel to the
horizon. Then, as if two loosened rims from the
disintegrating wheel were rolling into balance, mock
suns glowed hollowly at either end of the distended
hub.

Vena had moved close. Now, I realized, she was
holding to me, perhaps for reassurance, but maybe,
too, because of the utter loveliness of the refractive
spectacle. Then I found that I also had a tight arm
around her, perhaps because it was so chilly there by
the window.

The blaze in the heater was roaring against the red-
dened curve of the fire chamber, and the big teakettle
purred and spouted its swiftly condensing stream of
steam. Above them on a shelf an alarm clock ticked
the minutes away. The cabin was filled with homelike
smells, all the more stirring because of the eternal
booming and cracking and the hovering cold outside.

"Those are sun dogs," I said, and it didn't sound like
my voice. "I've never seen them before."

"They're so beautiful it's sort of frightening."

"When anything happens here," I said as I returned
the pressure of her hand, "I guess it always happens
big."

"What are you doing now?"

"Just getting my things together." I began to stow

compass, waterproof match case, knife, binoculars, and other hiking essentials in a small packsack.

"You're not going out?"

"Not today," I said.

The Aurora Borealis, a prodding battery of icy searchlights, was sweeping the night sky when I stepped outdoors that night to bring in one last log for the overnight fire. It seemed almost as if the northern lights were now so close that I could hear them, but the small, sharp, sudden rustlings just back of the stillness must have been my crystalizing breath.

For a moment I just stood there, attuned to the harmony of the universe. Rough, this weather? Just the opposite! What is more gratifying than the realization that you are proving yourself equal to the worst the elements have to offer? Did you ever notice that public opinion is a weak tyrant compared to our own private self-estimations?

"Comfortable?" I asked Vena when I came in with Bushman and made sure the latch was in place and the night fire secure.

"Oh, yes," she said from her bunk. "Did you look at the thermometer?"

"It's still about ninety degrees below freezing."

"It's like watching a ballet casting." She pulled her red-lined eiderdown sleeping robe over a round shoulder. "In a few days we'll hear on the radio about what they call a cold wave sweeping the States. Here we're watching it produced."

"I guess that's right."

"The weather will just be disagreeable in Chicago and New York and Boston, never dramatic like this." Her eyes met mine with their bright frank look. "You know, Brad, I'm discovering something. Living like this makes me forget the little things that don't really matter. That's good, isn't it, because most of the time it's hard to forget the little things."

"I suppose that's one reason I like the woods." Her

words kept moving through my head, and I stopped getting the cook stove's kindling ready for morning. "Actually, I never thought of it that way before. You're right, of course. All this does let one see how insignificant most of the small worries are."

"Most of the time I never even have time to think of them," she went on. In the illusive light that strained through the frosted windows, I could see her move her dark head. "That's strange itself, in a way, because here for the first time I have time for almost everything. Aren't you going to kiss me good night?"

"Since when have I forgotten that?"

"Darling," Vena said, "it's so cold tonight."

Trees, ice, and ground were cannonading with frost when I finally dropped off to sleep. But what brought me awake, twisting in the sweltering eiderdown, was the drip of water.

There was another sound that it took me a moment to isolate. The wilderness was stirring with the rollicking rhythm of wind.

"What's the matter?" came Vena's sleepy tones.

"Hear that?" I asked. Fresh air trickled pleasantly along my backbone, as I hunched up on one elbow.

"It sounds like water dripping from the roof."

I saw the frost was gone from the windows. Everything outside was varying shades of blue.

"That's right," I said. "The snow is melting."

"How can the snow be melting?" She sat upright, dark hair cascading prettily about her shoulders. "The cabin isn't on fire?"

"No, no," I said, and I laughed. "Everything's fine. It's chinooking."

8

First Chinook

The frost was gone. The night was clear and soft and filled with hundreds of stars that, in harmony with the tumult in the atmosphere, twinkled as if they were being twirled on jeweled pivots.

Still perspiring from the eiderdown, I stood in the open doorway and felt the warmness. Most of all, I felt the wind—balmy, springlike gusts of it swooping downriver from the west. The sound and the smell and the gentleness of it filled the reawakened wilderness.

"Water really is dripping," Vena said.

She was beside me now on the front stoop. I followed the line of her gaze to the eaves. I had on my boots, because if you automatically stepped into them when you got up, you were free to go anywhere, indoors or out. Vena had on hers, too. Her hand found mine, as we walked far enough out into the yard to see the shakes.

The snow was almost gone from these except where ice had formed a hard white hump along the lower edge of the roof. The shakes were deep black in the night. Water was flowing from them in sheets that the wind occasionally twisted and sometimes caught up in heavy spray that touched us wetly.

"Whatever is happening?" Vena said. Her eyes were

shining, and I heard her draw her breath in sharply. "The temperature is nearly fifty above."

Bushman was running round and around in a great circle, occasionally reversing his field. He was leaping bushes and logs and other obstructions, and he was barking.

"It's a chinook," I said, and I felt warm all over.

"Well, whatever it is," she said, "it makes me feel just like spring."

Living as I had in cities, I'd never thought much about the wind except as something that swept disagreeably along streets and around corners, lifting dust into my eyes. Here, heaving out of the night, the chinook wind peopled the darkness with vitality and friendliness. Shakes rattled. Trees creaked. Something kept banging, and I saw it was the Swede saw that I'd hung against the cabin on a spike.

"What's that rushing noise?" Vena asked, and she nodded in the general direction of the frozen brook.

A sheet of water was sluicing and splashing atop the ice, but I knew that wasn't what she meant. There was a nearby undertone to it all, a deeper sound that seemed to lift and ebb with the wind.

"It must be the waterfall," I said suddenly. "I wonder if we can see it? Let me get on a shirt."

Snow, no longer like gravel, was soft beneath our feet as we pressed toward a patch of small birch on the edge of the bank. Wind whipped at us, some of it as warm as a zephyr and then, in the same gust, so cold that it might have just brushed a glacier. It reminded me of standing in the foyer of a large Boston theatre, with cold wind prodding it from across the Common but being periodically thwarted by patrons opening one or another of the swinging doors and releasing gusts of heated air from inside. What was really happening now, I supposed, was that the mild chinook breezes were carrying with them the heavier air of the subzero snap.

"We'd better not get too close to the edge," I was saying. "It's pretty slippery."

"Look," Vena said, hand gripping mine again, "there it is."

Moonlight glowed from the heavy column of ice that, broadening as it plunged downward, reached from the plateau we were on to the river nearly a hundred feet below. Dancing water now bounced and splashed over this, catching the subtle light in a way that gave the impression of liquid fire.

"I'm hungry," Vena said abruptly, as if it were a discovery.

"So am I." Putting my arm around her as we walked back, I felt her shiver. "Hadn't you better go back to bed, though, and warm up? I forgot it's still winter."

"I couldn't go back to bed, not with all this."

"I guess I couldn't, either," I said. "You'd better get on something warmer, though. I'll start a fire in the cook stove."

Birch bark and dry spruce soon set the small stove to roaring. Then the additional homeliness of oatmeal plopping and bacon commencing to hop in a pan shoved the wind farther away. Vena was humming snatches of some little tune as she worked, her voice low and pleasant.

"What are you planning to do today?" she asked, a small bunch of silverware clanking in one hand as she lifted a side of the folding table.

"Why, I was thinking yesterday that we might go exploring," I said, glancing out at the swaying trees and streaming clouds, then back at her.

"Now that we've everything fixed for storing all the food that we'll be needing," she said carefully, "I wonder if it wouldn't be a good idea to go in soon for the rest of our supplies? You said that when the spring thaw comes, Ted Boynton won't be able to get through the mud for weeks."

The soft light of the approaching dawn struck her

hair as she moved about the stove. She had a ribbon holding it back, the same color as the red woolen robe that fitted her slimness, and with the bright flush in her cheeks she looked very pretty.

"You want to go to town, don't you?"

"Well," she said, and we both laughed. "It would be sort of nice to meet some more of the people, wouldn't it? And when I was down to Dudley's for mail last time, he spoke of a dance tonight. Today's Saturday, remember?"

"I guess it is," I said. "I'd lost count."

"I thought we might stay at the hotel tonight if you wanted," she went on, "and then ride back with Ted and the groceries tomorrow. Then I could go exploring with you. The weather will stay good that long, won't it?"

"I suppose so," I said, "but that doesn't make any difference. Now that spring is coming, there'll be plenty of good weather."

"I know you want to go along the river while it's still frozen."

"I imagine it would take a month of weather like this to thaw the river. Sure, we'll go to town today."

Other times when I had been in the woods, whenever I had wanted to go anywhere it had always been deeper into the wilderness. Now that we'd decided to go to Hudson Hope, though, I found myself beginning to look forward to it. A lot of this may have been due to the fact that Vena was so obviously pleased by the decision.

Wind puffed down the creaking stovepipe, starting smoke momentarily from the seams of the stove and depositing a powdery perimeter of ash around the lids. The wind created a great suction about the cabin, drawing out the warmth of the fire until, in a way, the air inside was chillier than it had been with the temperature a hundred degrees colder. The sound, the movement, and the balminess—like suddenly stepping out of a walk-in freezer into springtime—all stretched the nerves to an exquisite tautness.

"Breakfast is ready," Vena said, pouring the coffee.

What we could see of the wilderness from the four windows was beginning to silver with dawn. With this blending of night and day, the tumult of the wind quieted. The more familiar sounds of a warm winter morning became audible. Bushman was barking at swooping Canada jays. The clatter of running water suddenly reasserted itself. A coyote yelped. Two hunting owls exchanged their hoots. Drippings splattered from the roof.

"The chinook isn't over, is it?" Vena asked, and when I said I didn't think so, that it was probably just the wind's quieting as happened at dawn and again at dusk, she wanted to know what a chinook was.

I'd never experienced the lift of one before, either, but I'd heard and read of their sweeping across British Columbia and the Yukon, as well as other places. Here, I knew, they started from the Pacific Ocean as warm damp winds, so tempered by the Japanese Current that some of the lush valleys along the Canadian coast have a longer growing season than country far to the south, even around Birmingham, Alabama.

These heavy winds are further warmed by the process of losing their moisture in the mountains. Descending the far side of the heights, they are compressed and thus heated even more. By the time these snow-eaters, as the Indians call them, reach Hudson Hope, they are as clement as spring breezes.

It seemed as if everyone in Hudson Hope had been awaiting this change in weather to do the laundry. Towels and clothing whipped from a line Dudley Shaw had strung between a spruce and a small poplar. In about the same length of time again that it had taken us to reach Dudley's we came to the first log buildings of the small settlement, the several vacant cabins by themselves west of town. Then, about a half mile further downriver, the entire community emerged into sight; several dozen log cabins, with outstructures and occasional barns and pole corrals, all relaxing amiably around the red-roofed white buildings of one of the some 200 modern Hudson's Bay Company fur trading posts.

Fluttering, snapping laundry was in evidence everywhere. Its colors blended gayly with the browns and greys of the buildings, the off-white of snow and ice, and the green of bending spruce and lodgepole pine.

"The women have certainly been busy," Vena said.

The effect of her observation was spoiled somewhat when a short, rotund man, whom I later learned was Henry Stege who'd once had a trading post at Finlay Forks, appeared and began hanging out a seemingly endless line of woolen sox. Then Fred Monteith, another bachelor, appeared on the other side of the road and started going through the same procedure, although with long underwear. They both waved to us, and Henry Stege called out something.

"All right," Vena said to me. "Don't say it."

I was still a little afraid that Bushman might encounter trouble with the other dogs, which I'd read in books about the North are apt to be particularly ferocious. Dogs bustled out to meet him today. So far, though, he was having no difficulties, largely because in spite of his size he was still a puppy and was interested only in playing. Now he turned his frolicking attention toward some calves who were investigating a break in a fence around what seemed to be a garden. I yelled at him. Then a dog-wise cow charged him and sent him scurrying.

"Blasted things own the town," someone said.

Ted Boynton was leading one of his large horses out of his yard across from the hotel. The other horse followed along amicably.

"What?" I said.

"The cows," Ted said, "Peck's, Gething's, Kyllo's, and the rest of them. When the cattle aren't stirring up the mud and dust, the cayuses are. All this is free range in here, but Mrs. McFarland, Mrs. Rutledge, and the other ladies don't like it much when they look out the window and see the bull nipping the geraniums. Course, it's handy, though, to be able to buy milk and butter and to be able to ride when you don't hanker to walk."

"What's that about this being free range?" I asked.

"You can throw out your horses and cattle to graze whenever and wherever you want. It's up to the other folk to fence them out of where they're not wanted."

"They can get enough to eat by just grazing."

"Most of the horses can unless you're working them," Ted said, anchoring his stocking cap with one hand while he shoved some black hair under it with the other. "They'll keep in good shape, the majority of them will, on peavine, vetch, grass, and whatever else they take a fancy to. Cattle, of course, have to be fed through the cold months. Here, we put up oats and wild hay. That's why these critters are around town. Right now they're drifting down to the spring for water."

"We've been wondering about saddle horses," I said.

"While you were using them you'd have to toss them a couple of bundles a day," Ted said, shoving away the moist nose of the lead horse who was nuzzling his head. The horse pretended to nip in return. "That's oats. They sell for about a nickle a bundle, they do, depending on the crop. When the woods are green, of course, you could picket your horses where they can eat for free."

"What does a saddle horse cost?" Vena asked.

"All gentled and broke?" Ted readjusted his stocking cap as he started walking again, looking from one to the other of us. "Why, now, maybe forty dollars. That's a nice place for them up in the Canyon. You could ride about anywhere."

"Are there any around that we could buy?" Vena asked, and then she looked at me and added, "If we should want to, that is?"

"Well, now," Ted said, and he rubbed a square plump hand over that part of his thick hairy throat that glistened above high overalls between the unbuttoned halves of a faded flannel shirt. "The outfitters own most of the pack and saddle horses. They use them in season for hunting trips and survey parties. There's a fellow who's just moved to the Hope, though, who does some trading. Name is Gene Boring. He's setting up houskeeping in that last place on the right, across from Vic Peck's, as you're leaving town."

We were almost to the spring by now, and the two horses were pressing forward eagerly. The full warmth of the sun hit us as we turned with Ted and walked the short distance down the river slope to where a clear body of water, emerging among snow and sparkling icicles, gushed out of the ground with the intensity of a too-long confined brook.

It was one reason for Hudson Hope's having been built here, I knew. The other reason was that this was the foot of twenty-two-mile-long Rocky Mountain Canyon, only unnavigable portion of the Peace River in its otherwise tranquil course west to east through the backbone of the continent.

"Greetings!" someone called. I saw an otter-skin cap glistening from a bank on the opposite side of the rutted path to the river, where wooden steps led up to the side of the Hudson's Bay Company enclosure.

"Hi, Dave," I said.

"How's about a spot of coffee?"

Vena met my glance and nodded slightly, so I called back, "Thank you. Be right over."

"Next time, thanks," Ted was saying, squinting into the sun. "Just had some, Dave."

"Oh, by the way, Ted," I said, "can you drive us and some food from the Bay up to our place tomorrow?"

"Trail may be sort of soft with this chinook," Ted considered. "Do you reckon you'd mind leaving about daybreak so I can get back before it thaws too much? I could pick up your grubstake this afternoon, if that's all right, and be all set to head out when you get up."

"Daybreak will be fine," Vena said.

"Come on up this way," Dave Cuthill was saying, and the gate creaked as he swung it open. "Marion just put a fresh pot of coffee on the fire. No need to go all the way around."

The whole day was just as friendly, especially now that we had the thoughts of saddle horses to brighten our outlook even more.

One question often asked is whether newcomers to a wilderness area will be received in a friendly manner. If we'd had any misgivings, they wouldn't have lasted beyond that day and evening when we met a large proportion of our new neighbors; neighbors in such an outpost being everyone within five or fifty miles with whom you have any contact, perhaps only during an occasional meeting at the common outfitting center which in these woods was Hudson Hope itself.

The one dominant characteristic of these new neighbors of ours, we discovered, was their strong drive toward individuality. If they hadn't been individualists, the heads of the families at least wouldn't have been here in the first place. The independence and the necessary self-reliance of their day-by-day lives kept on making them all the more individualistic.

This proved to be particularly true of a place like Hudson Hope where, except for a few Cree and Beaver Indians who lived for the most part upwards of a day away to the south and north, there were scarcely any old families. There weren't, that is, in the sense of families that, as is not unusual in New England, had dwelt on their land for one or two centuries. Most of Hudson Hope's old-timers had come into the region at about the time of World War I. Mining, trapping, and ranching—sometimes a combination of all three— comprised their principal livelihoods.

The people we met were otherwise all different; some scrupulously neat, some too engrossed in varied interests to be essentially systematic, a few with sufficient ability for a dozen different executive positions, and others just hangers-on. But one thing all men and women alike had in common was a basic self-sufficiency, a habit of not even thinking of calling in a carpenter or a mason or even a doctor, but of taking care of themselves.

"Have you noticed something else, too?" Vena asked. "There's a tendency in those parts of rural New England where I've been, at least, of an indifferent regard of a man's own womenfolk as thinking human beings."

"I never noticed that," I said.

"You wouldn't, but it's there. I suppose that's one reason why I've tried so hard all my life, why I've disciplined myself and trained my mind and body into tools that could assure me some self-respect. But here the women are more like partners."

I had never realized that about her before, and I was interested.

"I don't suppose it's because anyone here is any more charitable or broadminded than the average person anywhere else," I said. "It's just the life."

There was a stalwartness to everyone, certainly, just as there must have been to earlier pioneers on this continent; although we soon found there was a slim handful locally that, for reasons of too frequent escapes in liquor, or because of laziness, or because of ineptitude, nothing but a frontier would have abided and let them eke out reasonable livings. Even these individuals did their useful tasks at times, when it became necessary, and so earned the few dollars it took them to exist.

In the big city they would have been charity cases or worse, whereas here they were among the kindliest and most colorful of the inhabitants. They were also the only individuals often available for the odd jobs that were all the time coming up, from digging a well to getting in a crop. The rest of the time, bothering no one and remaining sufficient unto themselves, they were respected as individuals, largely because, essentially, they themselves respected the integrity of others.

"It's fun meeting so many people, isn't it?" Vena said that afternoon when we were walking over to see Gene Boring about the horses. "And most of them are so interesting."

"That's partly because we're all so new to each other."

"Yes, but there's something else, Brad. Back in the city we tend to move for the most part among people of the same general age and interests. Everything is so hectic and crowded that we pretty much have to do that if we're going to have enough time to carry on our daily routine. Here, there's enough peace and room in which to regard people as the entities they are."

They were that, certainly, and there was an equality to what we could see of the community life that must have prevailed, too, when our present cities were also tiny clusters of cabins surrounded by mile upon spacious splendid mile of wilderness. There was little consciousness of class, largely because the dwellers here were all comparatively new to the country, without the hindrance or help of family backgrounds and past reputations, and with the space in which to expand in their own directions without infringing on anyone else.

"Just the kind of environment in which to make a new start the way you want to make it," was the way Vena summed it up. "I'm glad, though, that we live six miles from town. That way, the self-enclosed freshness can last a long while."

As we approached the cabin that Ted Boynton had said was Boring's, we saw a small, red-haired man striding toward several horses in an improvised corral. A halter was slung over one shoulder. He glanced around at Bushman's bark, and he waved a neighborly hand.

9

Dinosaur Tracks

"Fun?" Vena asked when, the previous night having culminated in a dance in a log building where Ted and Iva Boynton had at one time run a restaurant, we creaked back toward the cabin with Ted in a sleigh filled with supplies from the Hudson's Bay Company, gifts such as vegetables and preserves and game meat, and a welcome accumulation of mail. She looked happy.

"Fun," I agreed.

"It is still chinooking, isn't it?"

"It certainly is."

She threw back her head so the brisk morning wind, which near the river's edge had already bared sections of trail over which the metal runners grated and shrieked, rippled dark waves of hair away from her face.

"We ought to be able to make that trip of yours tomorrow, hadn't we?" When I nodded, she asked, "Where are we going, Brad?"

"Where would you like to go, Vena?"

Her hand gripped mine tight before she answered.

"Wherever you want. You must have some place in mind." She clasped her arms around herself. "It was nice getting to town, although I'm still glad we decided to live away from it. That way we can enjoy both places more. It'll be even better when we have saddle horses."

"You made out all right with Boring, I hear," Ted said.

"It sounds good, anyway," I said. "He told us we'd do better to wait until there's graze here before we bring in horses."

"Good idea," Ted nodded. "It'd be hard, anyway, to locate oat bundles this time of year."

"He says he has a sorrel and a grey on winter range at Beryl Prairie that are used to running together and that he thinks will be just right for us. He traded them recently from Don Peck and Pat Garbitt, he said. Do you happen to know anything about them, Ted?"

"The horses? No, Boring is all the time dickering."

"He said we could keep them awhile first and try them out," Vena said.

"Shouldn't go far wrong that way," Ted said.

Warm west wind, tossing the clusters of needles in the lodgepole pines, produced the same tranquil sound, swelling and then receding, as of a small waterfall splashing into a mountain meadow. Poplars squeaked as if with laughter. Whereas only a short time before they had been gauzed with frost, they now stretched in pearl grey nakedness against a deep blue sky.

"How long will it last, Ted?" Vena was saying.

"The chinook," I added.

"Hard to say." He shoved a willow twig between small teeth, and the movement of his button mouth brought back a twist of good-humored jollity to his face. "Some winters here, now, aren't much more than one chinook after another. But this chinook? Well, the barometer was still low this morning, so it should stay awhile yet."

"I always thought a low barometer meant a storm."

"Not here, it don't, Brad," Ted said. "It don't unless the wind is cutting out of the north. Get a low barom-

The ice became even smoother. Much of the way now it was an almost flawless sidewalk from one shore to the other. We passed a point on the south bank where the blackness of a coal seam was exposed.

"That must be what they call Contact Point," I said.

~~were other creeks, one with a frozen waterfall~~

eter and a downriver wind here any time of the year, and you're in for some real fine weather. Fact is, you can tell if a chinook's coming even without a barometer by watching horses and cattle. They begin to get high-spirited and frisky half a day or so ahead of time."

He chuckled.

"People, too, sometimes," he said, tightening the left rein and swinging the grating sleigh in a wide arc beside our brook. "Here we are. I'd better help you unload and get started back before it thaws any more."

The wind quieted during the next night. It was with a certain amount of apprehension that, in the still of the early morning darkness, I shone a flashlight on the thermometer. The temperature, although lower, was still a pleasant 42° above. The barometer, where I next directed the beam, remained down.

Bushman, barking, was romping around outside. I waited until kindling began snapping in the stove, set in heavier split pine, adjusted the filled teakettle over the hole, and went back to bed.

"Time to get up?" Vena asked sleepily.

"We may as well wait for the water to start boiling."

Then I had to get up, anyway, to let Bushman in. He planted his wet feet on my chest in such good spirits that I couldn't help answering his invitation to wrestle. Then he bounced across to Vena and kept nuzzling her neck and shoulders until she decided to get up, too. We were both laughing, and Bushman kept frisking from one to the other of us, growling with pretended ferocity.

Vena laughed jubilantly, rescuing the belt of her red robe.

"Oh, it's going to be a wonderful day," she said. "I can just feel it. Let's hurry and get ready."

I recall, when I was a youngster, attending a special matinee where Thornton W. Burgess, who wrote about Peter Rabbit and Jimmy Muskrat and their friends,

was making a personal appearance. One thing I've always remembered is how few hands went up when Mr.
Burgess inquired who among us had seen a sunrise. I
thought now, if he'd asked that question of any Far
Northern audience, there never would have been such
a sparcity of uplifted palms. With sunrises during the
Hudson Hope year taking place from shortly before
noon in the winter to soon after midnight during the
summer, it is almost impossible not to see a good many
of them.

In any event, except in the city, partly because there
it was the comparatively undisturbed nights that
seemed the best for writing, I had always liked to get up
while the day was new. There were so many things to
do and enjoy here that few days seemed long enough.
This morning we watched dawn quickening the world
while we were walking up the Peace River.

"Isn't it blue?" Vena said.

The channel, smoothed by water over the years,
bounded by the shore itself and then by greyish cliffs
and yellowish cut banks and finally by wooded hills,
was like a long trough. The air that had settled in this
depression, heavier and damper than that in the sur-
rounding atmosphere, was so intensely blue that it
seemed like liquid dye. The deepest coloration was
along the river itself. Above this, the colors gave up
saturation and gained brilliance as they modified
through powder blues, lilacs, and mauves until finally
diminishing into pinks.

High clouds behind us in the east, radiant with the
still hidden sun, were serene golds and yellows against
a pale azure sky too remote to be influenced by the
earth-bound river. Lower wind-driven clouds, streaming from the purple west toward the carnation-pink
east, became drenched with the hues characteristic to
their elevations.

The snow and ice of the Peace River was enlivened
by deep blue reflections that took possession of rippling

Dinosaur Tracks

pools and streaks of overflow. Green water occ
ally hurtled from beneath the enslaving ice for a 1.
burst of freedom before being imprisoned again.
wind licked spray from huge icicles, the frozen outp
of springs, that pillared cliffs opposite the cabin.

"What are those, Brad?" The words broke in on

"It gives one a funny feeling to be walking on them, doesn't it?"

The mine lay just above, a few feet from the river. We started into one tunnel, but it only led a short way. The next one we tried vanished somewhere among the shadows within the mountain, but after a few yards the lower part became clogged with frozen drainage. The third tunnel we essayed, however, seemed clear.

"Here, Bush," I called.

"There he is, outside," Vena said. "I guess he doesn't care too much for it in here."

Bushman was running back and forth in the patch of daylight behind us and barking. He came to me finally. Reaching down a hand to pat him, I could feel him shivering.

"Heel," I said.

For a few moments there was only the rasp of the dog's nails, an occasional rush of panting, and a grunt when once he missed his footing and slipped against me. Then he was gone again and was once more outside, barking.

"He'll be all right out there," Vena said. "We're not going in much further, anyway, are we?"

"We can only see a little way more. Next time we'll have to bring a flashlight."

She didn't reply.

Daylight pressed weakly after us. It showed a low passage extending back under Bullhead Mountain. Where the black floor was not as thick with ice as elsewhere, short ties marked where narrow tracks, since removed, had once extended. The ice, whose succession of rounded edges suggested that it had frozen while seeping down the barely perceptible grade, reflected the diminishing light.

"Isn't that driftwood?" Vena said.

I'd noticed where sticks and twigs had been wedged between the walls and some of the posts supporting the roof. Now I saw that some of the larger pieces were so stuck that they could only have been lodged in place from the direction of the Peace.

"The river must have flooded sometime," I said. "I guess it can get pretty rugged during high water some years. Say, I wish we could see some of those fossils King Gething was talking about in town."

"It's pretty dark for that."

"Well, we can't get lost, anyway."

"No," Vena said, "but I've heard about dangerous gas in old mines."

"There can't be very much in this particular tunnel. Don't you feel that fresh draft in our faces?"

"Yes, I guess I do." The single passage was beginning to curve, and her fingers caught mine. "It must be getting late. I'd like to see everything before we have to go back."

"All right," I said. "We can't do anything in here without more light, anyway."

It was easier returning, with daylight ahead of us. Bushman, frisking and jumping, bounded about us when we stood among the dinosaur tracks again.

"We can come back later," I said, "and bring a flashlight. I'll bring that little prospector's pick of mine, too. Now we'd better have that look around and get started back."

The strong chinook wind, blowing on our backs, made the return trip even quicker than we'd expected. We could see the river slanting downhill now. Sometimes, when we took a running start and slid, we spread our jackets open like sails to give us added impetus. Bushman skidded and barked after us.

The late afternoon turned to a deep, intense blue as we traveled. When a full moon lifted ahead of us, huge at first because of the magnifying atmosphere, it was like something out of a dream. I felt as if I were expanding and as if the beauty was pouring into me until it filled my body to the brim.

Then relaxed and pleasantly heavy with fatigue, yet so buoyant with the magnificence of the night that it was as if our very feet were floating, we followed the scrambling Bushman up the bank, occasionally grasping his tail for support. Ahead gleamed the log walls that spoke of sanctuary and shelter.

"I hate to go indoors," Vena said.

"So do I."

We stood there a few minutes more, in the warm wind and the star-pointed yellow moonlight, listening to the breezes and the water and the occasional forest life, smelling the conifers and the aroma of the freshly bared land, joined by a mutual appreciation that freed us to each other. The wolfhound was the only one who seemed puzzled, and then he whined.

"Poor Bush is hungry," Vena said.

The cabin, the redolence of its newness released by the lingering heat of the sun, was warm and welcoming when we entered. But it was the man-made light, that pin prick in infinity resulting from the touch of a match to a coal oil wick, that brought us all the way back.

We talked. We ate. Finally, we slept, as carefree as if on a school day holiday years before. When I awoke in the quiet of the next morning, it was to pull the eiderdown higher about my ears. Cold had descended again.

10

Ours for the Eating

"Where are you going with that shovel?" Vena asked me.

"What's left of that moose quarter Dudley gave us is thawing," I said. "I want to wrap it to keep it dry and then bury it in that snowbank across the creek."

"Will it keep that way?"

"It should be all right for a couple more weeks."

"How about Bushman?" she asked. "That dog is a walking appetite."

"He's just a growing boy. Anyway, I'm going to nail the meat inside a wooden box first."

Vena was occupied at the table by the windows, with letters and stationery spread before her, and now she turned toward the large Hudson's Bay Company calendar.

"Do you know the date?" she started. Then she said in a different voice, "Darling, do you know what day this is?"

"Now I do. It's the first day of spring."

"You sound sorry that spring is here."

"It isn't that." I was getting a piece of plastic sheeting from my shelves. "I guess I just sort of hate to think that winter is over. It's been a good winter."

"Our first winter in the woods," she said.

"Yes. Everything here so far has been so good that I don't like to see any of it passing. When you come down to it, one year doesn't last very long."

"So we shouldn't waste any of it," she said suddenly. She capped her fountain pen while rising to her feet. "Let's go for a walk during the first dusk of spring. We can, can't we? You don't have anything else to do? Oh, the meat. How long will it take you to fix that?"

"I'll do it tomorrow."

We found pussy willows downriver in a rocky niche where a spring seeped out of the north bank and where, sheltered, the slender red wands could expand in both direct and reflected sunlight. The little grey ovals appeared to gleam, the moisture on their platinum pelage glistening like miniature opals in the fire of the sunset.

"I never expected to find anything like this in March so far north," Vena said. "They're so beautiful I hate to pick them. But it would be nice to have a bit of spring in the cabin."

"They'll be coming out everywhere. Here, I can probably reach those."

They seemed to shine in my hand. Bushman bounded close for a sniff, then bounced away disinterested. Now that the willows were close, we could see how some of the crystalline droplets, caught like spangles in the silvery hair, acted like miniature lenses, magnifying the delicate strands that supported them.

After that we were silent for awhile, as if it were enough to stroll on the frozen river while the birds took care of any conversation. Even Bushman followed silently at our heels. We crossed the Peace, finally, and turned slowly back so as to have the sunset before us. Blazing in its horizon haze, the sun nicked the rim of the world.

What breeze remained was in the tops of the pines and poplars on the cut bank high above. When, as if far away, these trees occasionally squeaked, it was as if the earth was creaking on its axis. This illusion became all the stronger when I realized that it was only because this axis was slanting more and more toward the sun that we had come into the spring season at all.

It wasn't that the earth was any closer to the sun, for in points of miles the two were actually farther apart after the vernal equinox, that moment when the sun is at right angles to the equator and when everywhere on this globe night and day are of equal length. It was that throughout the spring the sun shines more directly on the northern hemisphere, so that there is less heat-absorbing atmosphere to cool its rays. By the end of spring, the sun would be scorching the North Pole one-fifth more hotly than it would be the Equator.

"With the weather becoming warm," Vena said suddenly, "I should be able to begin helping more with our living expenses."

"You're doing fine now. I want you to enjoy yourself. Besides, what extra firewood you burn doesn't cost us anything but a little work."

"I didn't mean that." I thought she looked at me suspiciously. "But now that springtime is here, won't all those wild foods we've been hearing about start growing?"

"That's right. I guess they should be."

"As a matter of fact," she said, and she turned the pussy willows in her hand, "don't you suppose that some of them are up already? Let's take tomorrow off, Brad, and go looking. I'd like to get out all day, anyway. It's much too nice to stay indoors, even in a log cabin."

We packed Bushman the next morning for the first time. A large flour sack, sewn back together at the end and then slit open across the middle of one side, provided his pack. Vena had sewn on a canvas strap to go over his head and to keep the whole thing from sliding backwards. When this pack was laid over Bush's back, it afforded two pockets.

We loaded it lightly with lunch and tea pail, and then we covered it with a rectangle of waterproof canvas for protection. The wolfhound did not seem to know what to make of it all. Instead of trying to lie down as we'd heard many dogs did at first, however, he kept rearing up on his hind feet. While Vena steadied and patted him, I roped everything snug. Then, watching him closely, we let him go. After a few hops, he seemed to forget anything was different. As insurance, though, we left a rope trailing from his collar that, in case he should start off after a rabbit, we would have a chance of grabbing.

"Heel," I said.

Bushman heeled enthusiastically. Happily, he followed us away from the cabin, eager to be off on another excursion.

"Now we can pick up a few groceries whenever we go to Hudson Hope for the mail," Vena said, "and we won't have to carry anything."

"Not even the mail," I agreed.

"Dhulart dun Delgan will be earning his keep, too," she agreed. "That leaves it up to me."

We had been looking all winter at the long slopes across the river. The past few days these had been luring us more than ever, particularly as we could see large stretches becoming more and more bare.

With much of the area spread out before our cabin windows like a vast relief map, we had laid out our route so as to avoid as much snow as possible. I had sketched a map on the page of a notebook, showing bare ridges and slopes, darkening in expanses of tall thick spruce under which snowfall would lie thinly, and marking compass directions. Now we headed down the pitch to the river and across the ice toward the other side.

"Aren't you afraid of becoming lost?" a friend wrote us soon after our arrival. "I know I should be, especially now that I've found Hudson Hope on the map.

Why, where you are, in the corner east of Alaska and below the Yukon border, you could actually wander for hundreds of miles and never come to any kind of a road. You must have some safeguard."

We did. It was a compass.

With a compass, as I'd gone over carefully with Vena who now also always carried one, you could wander anywhere in the world and always find your way back. Having a map of where you were, as we did, made it all the easier. What if we didn't happen to have that map handy? Then we could always draw one as we traveled. Even the most experienced explorers used exactly the same method, although in their cases the map might take form in their minds.

To make it easy, as I explained to Vena, you really need a compass, watch, map, and pencil. Every ten minutes, or every time you change direction, will not be too often at first to bring that map up to date. No map? Then sketch one as you go. Distances? Measure them by the time it takes to travel them.

Later on, all this information can be carried in the mind. The formula, however, always remains the same. We can always tell where we are in relation to where we started by timing ourselves or otherwise measuring the distances covered, and by making a visual or mental record of all the angles of travel.

"That sounds simple," Vena said after thinking it over.

"It is simple. It just requires a little work and concentration in the beginning, that's all."

With the Peace River running from west to east through this entire country, we could hardly stay lost as long as we could travel. If we were on the cabin side of the river, all we had to do any time was head south to reach the water. If we were across river, walking north would bring us back.

There was a trick of the trade, of course. Instead of trying in unfamiliar surroundings to come out exactly

at the cabin, we found time would be saved by bearing
definitely upriver or downriver of it. Then upon reaching the stream, we would know for sure which way to
turn.

But the point is, there was no real danger. Once we
realized we could wander wherever we pleased and still
always be sure of getting safely back, I felt a whole lot
freer than I had at any other time in my life.

"When will the ice go out?" Vena asked, as with
Bushman behind us we reached the south shore.

"Not for over a month, Dudley says. I guess it must
be quite a spectacle."

"I'm looking forward to it," she said. She caught my
right hand and brought it around her, leaning back
against my shoulder with her face close to my cheek.
"What a story we'll have to tell when we get back
home to Boston!"

I didn't say anything, not even when she drew a deep
breath and stirred. I was thinking that for me this was
more home than any I had ever known before.

About a quarter mile down the river from where our
cabin gleamed on the opposite flat, a small waterfall
made a short glinting column in a patch of woods a
few yards in from the river. We scrambled up a game
trail, held in place by exposed tree roots, on the east
side of this fall and followed the brook inland.

"Am I seeing things?" Vena asked.

She pointed at where Bushman, who'd slipped into
the bush to investigate what I saw were fresh coyote
tracks, now stood a few feet ahead of us where the
brook gurgled in a silvery loop. His dark grey head was
cocked, and he seemed to be regarding the singing
water.

Then I saw it, too. A small bird, darkish and stubby,
was walking on the bed of the stream. Its unhesitating
feet, which were unwebbed and ordinary enough, as-
cended a slanting rock until, without changing stride,

the slate-colored bird was above the water again. I thought it would shake itself or at least preen its feathers. All it did, though, was twist its head with brief unconcern in our direction, bob several times in the process of walking, and then as matter-of-factly pace down the other side of the rock and beneath the surface once more.

"It's a water ouzel. Some people call them dippers."

"How does it keep its footing? That water is fast." She gave a little shiver. "And cold."

"I don't know. You'd think it would use its wings."

The short-tailed little bird appeared again, almost below Bushman, with what looked like some sort of dripping insect in its mouth. It held the object in its beak, straightened its neck, and swallowed. Then it sang a few notes that were clear and liquid like water gurgling over pebbles, skimmed the surface of the water with a swift beating of wings, and disappeared around a bend, leaving Bushman too engrossed even to bark.

We came to where the brook had frozen in a series of levels, where rocks and fallen trees had dammed its winter overflow. It was like ascending an icy staircase. We kept climbing up and up into the hills. The steps became so high along one narrow canyon, where there was little surface moisture to take away the slipperiness, that I took Vena's mittened hand to steady her.

Her face was a little flushed because of the cold air that, now that the upper atmosphere was warming and lifting, was spilling down this chasm. Long brown hair was twisting about her face, and she backhanded it gracefully. The attractiveness of the gesture made me realize again how well she looked in plaid ski pants, brown flannel shirt, and a red eiderdown jacket, even though this last had more bulk than shape.

"What are you thinking?" I asked.

"That it's spring," she said, "and yet it doesn't feel like spring."

"It's cold down in here, but wait until we get up out of this cut. Heel, Bushman."

The wolfhound was having his usual trouble in keeping his footing. His large feet splayed, seeking traction, and his nails rasped on the ice. Now and then he stopped and bit at frozen snow that accumulated among his toes, tearing out offending tufts of hair as he did so. At the moment, trending toward the snow that along this particular stretch powdered one side of the stream, he had stopped at some saucerlike tracks and was alternately sniffing ground and air. I grabbed the trailing rope, then his collar.

"What is it, Brad?"

"A lynx. See?"

The long-legged, grey leanness of the big cat was flowing along a hare run. We were standing motionless when it turned and tried to make us out. Its stub of a tail switched tensely from side to side. Then Bushman pulled me a step ahead, and it padded away.

"Will it come back?" Vena asked.

"Not likely."

"You're laughing at me. But it gave me a funny feeling, didn't it you, when it was looking at us. And that tail!"

"It was just trying to make us out. It couldn't smell us with the wind blowing the way it is. They live on varying hare. We'd better keep hold of Bushman's rope for awhile.

"Are lynx good to eat?"

"Oh, yes. Any animal is good to eat, and Dudley says they taste like the white meat of chicken. Why, are you getting hungry?"

"No, I was just thinking of the reason we came today."

"That's right. We should be finding some edible plants soon."

We finally reached an ascending series of open poplar benches, where bluffs lifted on either side of the brook beyond steep, spruce-greened banks. I tried vainly to make out the cabin through the trees, but although I could mark where it was, it blended in too well with the forest.

"Here's where we could see from the windows," I said. "We turn south here."

A game trail, hardened by moose and deer hoofs and smoothed by the pads of smaller game, provided an easy way upward. We finally found ourselves in an ancient canyon that widened, then narrowed, and finally broadened again before us.

"The Peace, or some other river, must have come this way centuries ago," I said. "I wonder if it left any placer gold here?"

Vena, examining a patch of greenery, didn't seem to hear.

The walls on either side of us now were some eighty feet high and consisted of water-smoothed rock, although the present bed of the Peace was at a considerably lower elevation. In this dimness, the light seemed to cup upward from the snowdusted ground rather than downward through the spruce boughs that rustled heavily overhead. The cool beauty was somehow warming in its serenity.

"What's been at that tree?"

The giant poplar at which Vena was pointing—and when Alexander Mackenzie had gone through this country, the much-traveled explorer had noted that these were the largest poplar trees he'd ever seen—had been so deeply chewed around its base that the core still supporting it was less than a foot across.

"A beaver."

"They must be wonderful," she said. "I've read how they can fell a tree wherever they want it to go."

"Well, not exactly. What they mostly do is chew away at trees that, being on slopes near ponds and creeks, naturally fall into the water. Actually, they just worry round and around until something gives—like a lot of people."

Light ahead, indicating a clearing, grew brighter as we walked on. Presently, we saw through the trees a shallow hollow among the hills. Sheeted with ice, this was crisscrossed with low brown dams and dotted in several places with the brown mounds of beaver lodges. Although we held Bushman and tried to approach quietly, a not too difficult task in the soft snow, there was a startling smack as we got closer.

"Do they actually make that warning sound by hitting the water with their tails?" Verna asked. "It sounded more like a rifle shot."

"Yes, that's where he was working." A poplar tree near where open water rippled between shore and ice had a deep white notch, and the snow about it was dark with chips. "He's probably back under his house by now. Let's have a look."

It was necessary to step over a perimeter of open water, where the heat daily being absorbed by the earth had done its melting, but after that the ice was fine. That the pond was shallow was attested to both by the configuration of the land and by the willows and bulrushes that poked their way here and there through the white sheath.

"When the young shoots of both of those begin coming up," I said, "their insides will be good to eat."

Pussy willows growing from the dome of the larger of three beaver lodges gave a sense of spring to the still wintry scene. These houses, we could see at close range, were made of sticks and mud, their crude strength reminding me of primitive art. A cable of moose tracks, frozen where overflow sometime during the winter had welded slush to the ice, circled the lodge at which Bushman was sniffing and, vanishing among the brown cattails, tied it to the greening shore.

"What's that green over there?" Vena asked.

"Kinnikinic," I said. "We see it growing above the Hope when we're coming downriver."

"Isn't that good to eat, too?"

"Well, they say the bear like it in the spring. I've tried it, though, and there isn't much taste to either the leaves or the berries. What the early pioneers used to do is dry the leaves and pulverize them for a tobacco substitute. We should be able to find something better."

We kept climbing short slopes, following benches inland for distances varying from a few hundred feet to half a mile, and then climbing again. I lost count of all the deer we saw, and we came upon about a dozen moose. That noon we boiled the kettle and toasted our sandwiches atop the high ridge following the south side of the Peace.

Just behind, a small frozen lake shone in the sun. Upriver of it was the flat top of Mount Gething. Across the river and slightly to the left as we faced or tree-hidden cabin was Bullhead Mountain. Its broad bulk stood out so formidably and so near at hand that it seemed odder than ever that we couldn't see it from either our homesite or from Hudson Hope. Beyond, arrowing northward and cut from Bullhead by the narrow gap along which ran the portage road, was the sunny Butler Range.

We had nearly filled a bag with dandelion greens on the way up, and I had found some young nettles on a sunny damp expanse sheltered by deadfall. Gloves and my sharp knife had made the gathering of these small green shoots uneventful, although I could see that Vena remained a little doubtful. It was on the way home that afternoon that we made our big find, although my wife was even less convinced that she had been with the nettles.

"Skunk cabbage?" she repeated.

"Yes," I said. "It's a bit hard to recognize, isn't it, but I remember it from when I was a boy. It's one of the first plants to come up toward the end of winter."

"I don't doubt you," she said, kneeling beside me where the compactly folded leaves, sheathed in brownish purple hoods, were shoving their way through frost-sheeted leaf mold. "But eating it?"

"That's what I thought, too. When it's young like this, though, it's delicious."

11

The Shining Highway

That evening Vena brought the lush, moist wild cabbage leaves with their pale thick stalks to the boiling point in three changes of water to remove all hints of strong odor. Then she seasoned them with salt, pepper, and melting blobs of yellow margarine.

The nettles, of which we had all too few, cooked up with even less bother. Merely dropping them in a very small amount of boiling salted water, which Vena immediately moved to the back of the stove, quickly wilted them and removed all traces of sting. As soon as the liquid had cooled sufficiently to sip, she added golden daubs of oleomargarine.

As for the dandelions, these were so young and tender that Vena concocted a vinegar dressing of her own and served them as salad.

After weeks without fresh vegetables and with already robust appetites stimulated by a long day outdoors, it really took will power to wait until everything was on the table. The sun had set long ago, but traces of it still livened clouds upriver. I held Vena's chair for her, then stepped around Bushman and settled into my own. The food smelled delicious.

"It looks almost too good to eat," I said, "all that red moose meat against the white of potatoes and the green of the vegetables."

"Maybe it won't taste as good as it looks."

She just sat there, fork in hand, watching me. I sampled the nettles first, partly because of a habit I've long had of getting the less agreeable parts of a meal, such as spinach, out of the way at the beginning. But the nettles had a delicate aroma, as I could tell when the dark, moist forkful approached my lips. The taste was delicate, like the fragrance of meadow land on a sunny spring day.

The skunk cabbage had none of the harsh overtones of domestic varieties. Automatically, my fork slid among the crisp bright leaves of the dandelion salad. The clean, slightly bitter crunchiness set off the subtlety of the other two wild vegetables.

I could feel myself smiling and chewing at the same time, as I looked up to see how Vena was enjoying her own share. It was only then that I realized she was so intent on my reaction that she hadn't yet eaten a thing.

"It does taste good, though," I said.

She looked particularly pretty in the soft light, her coloring fresh from the day in the hills and the last radiance of the day picking out shadows in her brown hair.

"Maybe it's just because you're hungry."

"It's delicious. How can you tell until you try it?"

She seemed almost afraid as she stirred the nettles a bit to distribute the seasoning, then doubtfully lifted a small green wad. Her expression had lost even more of its tension by the time she sampled the cabbage.

"See?" I said. "Anyway, it isn't that important."

She avoided my look until she'd decided for herself about the salad, too. Then she glanced up swiftly, her eyes shining almost the way they had back in the Newbury Street restaurant that snowy afternoon when we had made our decision to come to the woods. I thought for a moment she was going to cry.

"It is terribly important," she said.

There was a catch in her voice, but then she forced a laugh.

"You don't know how it's been, having everything done for me and being so helpless. Now, I can help, too."

"Why, you've been a wonderful help from the start."

"I still can't even bake bread decently," she said.

"Well, it's getting better all the time."

"And I don't know anything about this sort of life. You've had to help me every step of the way. I guess I'm too accustomed to taking care of myself."

Her teeth were on her unsteady lower lip.

"I thought this was a partnership," I started.

"That's just it," she said. "That's why all that's been happening has made me feel so helpless. But now I can have a share in things. While you're busy, I can find us all sorts of things to eat. Then, later, there'll be my garden. That's why I wanted a garden."

When I kissed her, she threw her arms tightly around me for a moment.

"I'm all right now. We'd better eat before all this gets cold."

Then we were talking and laughing between mouthfuls. Afterwards, I pushed back contentedly from the table so I could stretch out my legs. Bushman got up at the movement, and I put down a hand and scratched behind his ears the way he liked.

"This is just the beginning," I told her. "You'll be amazed at all the different wild foods that will be springing up. We'll learn lots of local ones from Dudley, Ted, King, and the others. Why, if we wanted, we could live entirely off the country."

"Why don't we?"

"Mostly because it would mean such a disproportionate amount of work. It's easier in this civilization to work at something else long enough to earn the price of things like flour and lard."

"How could we make our own flour?"

"Well, if we didn't want to bother with the wild grains and such, we could dry and powder something like the inner bark of the birch tree. That's particularly nourishing. It helped save a lot of people from starving during the Civil War and other emergencies. Then there's those bulrushes we saw today. The insides of the roots can be dried and ground."

"All right, how about lard?" I could see she was enjoying herself.

"There's rendered bear fat, for one. Dudley and the others I've talked to say it's even better than commercial lard to cook with, especially for things like pies."

"You're going to get us a bear, aren't you?"

"I hope so. They must be out of hibernation."

"I want to learn everything I can about all those foods, starting right now," Vena said. "I don't care how much work it is for me. I want to cook with all of them we can. It can be my share. You've been doing too much. Why, when we came away, you even had to help me shop for the right kind of clothes."

"Why, that's been what I've always liked about us," I said. "We've always been able to share everything."

"Don't you see?" she said. "I want to share, too. I don't care how rough anything is just so long as I can share it with you."

Now that the new season was upon us, the rapidly lengthening hours of daylight so hurried it that in some respects we were ahead of more southerly portions of the continent. Rising water kept cutting through the layers of ice in our brook until, beside the cabin where the sun hit, I finally had to chop steps so I could get down to fill our buckets.

"Have you looked outdoors lately?" Vena asked me one morning when I was busy at the typewriter.

The stream had flooded suddenly, and a muddy torrent was clearing away chips by the woodpile. We went out and moved some of the wood so it would be out of danger. Then we walked inland a way along the shallow groove Bull Creek had worn out of the wilderness.

"If it weren't for the bushes, and the deadfall, and the beaver dams," I told Vena, "I could pole a small canoe all the way back to the hills."

"When will the river go out, I wonder?" she said when we'd returned and were standing on the cliff, looking at where the brook's muddy torrent was splashing down onto the ice and filling hollows and depressions with turbid water.

"Dudley says it will be a few more weeks."

"I wonder what it will be like? It should be spectacular."

Our preconception may have come from fiction, I suppose, for what we expected was a roaring rise of water that would sweep everything before it in a crashing, jamming mass of ice. The actual breakup, however, was extreme only in its gradualness.

For a month after the change to warm weather, the ice continued to lie in a vast glaring sheet over the Peace River. The major change, at first, was in its color. White turned grey, as the snows melted and left the actual ice bare.

The frozen expanses dulled, as dust that had swept onto them through the winter months became exposed. This coating became thicker with the appearance of increasing layers of the dust which, in turn, absorbed more of the sun's rays and thus hastened the process. Where occasional rocks pocked the surface, the decomposition proceeded at an even faster pace. Brown and yellowish chunks of stone and shale soon lay in craters of their own insistence.

With cold nights following warm days, the surface meltings filled crevices and cemented cracks, making the entire body of ice flatter and apparently more solid. Nevertheless, we traveled the river with increasing caution, testing any doubtful places well ahead of us with the long poles we always carried so that, if we ever should break through, the horizontally held pole could be reasonably counted upon to bridge solid ice and thus afford an escape.

The shining highway, winding smoothly through rough and still drifted country, kept calling irresistibly. Afternoons we were generally outdoors with Bushman, exploring the islands, the sheer banks inaccessible other times of the year, and the occasional frozen streams that twined back among the hills. We followed many of these latter on our regular forays inland after the increasing variety of wild edibles.

Young fireweed began coming up and proved to be delicious. Plantain, which we'd often seen as one of Massachusetts' most common weeds, also quickly boiled into excellent greens, while the younger of them made delicately flavored salads. We tried clover leaves in salad, and the easily identified three-leaflet perennial proved superior in that department. Tastiest of the greens that were new to us, however, was pigweed. Vena liked this all the better, I think, when she discovered that another common name for it is lamb's-quarters.

The ice started to candle in places, to disintegrate into masses of long vertical needles. These, Dudley had warned us, were so treacherous that a man could step on a seemingly safe portion and plunge through as abruptly as through crusted snow. Where this candling seemed most prevalent, however, was in shallow areas where the warming land added its onslaught to that of the direct sunlight. We became more and more cautious.

For awhile there was a period of colder weather, and the water level lowered considerably. Water did continue to break up the more quickly rotting shore ice, but by following the reef in front of our cabin to the heavy concentration of ice that formed a broad band in the center, it was reasonable to make our way up and down the river for another two weeks.

Occasionally we were stopped by what looked like

brawling new rivers. These spumed up from under the ice and cut deepening channels along its surface before disappearing into turbulent holes. If it wasn't easy to go around these surface streams, however, it always proved possible to cross on stranded ice cakes or by cautious wading. For the most part, these cascades waxed and waned with the daytime warmth. They were often no more than trickles that smiled along worn grooves when we set out in the morning. By our return in late afternoon, however, they had often grown to roaring sluiceways that glared with a thousand glittering eyes.

Bushman dragged a long manila rope these days, both so that we would have a chance of hauling him to safety if he should fall in and so it could act as a safety line in case either of us should need help. The icy sidewalk had a fascination for me, especially as I realized we soon would be forced back to the comparatively tedious, thawing, softening, and still largely snow-covered land.

A warm west wind started to blow again. Then the inexorable pressure of rising water, forcing its way through suddenly inadequate channels, really began making itself felt. Ice buckled, split, broke, and eventually mashed into jumbled cakes. Slush frosted the spaces between these, so deceptively that one day Bushman jumped atop one of these white masses while following us to the still solid ice a few feet out from shore.

"Watch out," Vena called.

Luckily, he was beside me, and I managed to grab his collar and yank him to solid footing. He picked his way to shore and shook himself dry with a certain injured dignity. Then he turned his back on the river and stood there, pretending to examine water gushing from the flat above onto the remnants of the frozen waterfall.

"Soaked," I said, quickly going through the contents of his pack. "The nincompoop."

"Had we better go back while I put up some fresh sandwiches?" Vena asked, stroking the grey head which maintained a studied indifference, although the long grey tail gave a minor sort of wag.

"I hate to say it," I said, "but I guess the really smart thing will be to go back and stay on this side of the Peace from now on. This is getting a little too rambunctious. I could have stepped in that slush as easily as Bushman. It did look solid."

Whether or not at the mention of his name, Bushman's tail gave a long sweep.

Almost before we noticed it that week, parts of river began to break free along the surface cascades. Cakes would tumble, grate, crash, pile, and slide together at the end of a flowage, effectively blocking the exit funnel. Eventually the rising water would float this dam aside, and the whole process would commence again. Further upriver, the wider and shallower expanse of river opened up, then was dammed by a tremendous jumble of ice in Box Canyon behind which the slush-sparkling flood rose higher.

Box Canyon finally opened just before the first of May with a thunderous surge that started Bushman barking and brought us running to the edge of the cliff. The sun was setting, and the spinning, bobbing cakes became carmine chips tossing in a gigantic crimson gutter.

The flooded expanse above Box Canyon having drained during the night, the swollen torrent had subsided by the time we went out to look at it the next morning.

"Look at those," Vena said.

On the slanted rockiness of the great reef below were stranded a half dozen huge blocks of ice, several of them as tall and broad as small cottages.

"And we were worrying," I said, "about whether the ice was thick enough to hold us."

"They're so big. How will they ever melt?"

"Maybe we'll be able to go down in July," I said, "and chip off ice cubes."

What happened, though, was that the river swelled a final time, with the sustained May melt, and started bearing them away. The hurtling brilliance of ice cakes of every size was now joined with silt, bushes, jagged limbs, saplings, and, eventually, huge trees whose gnarled roots lifted and turned cumbersomely in the torrent. I found myself pausing for hours beside the river, fascinated by the ever-changing spectacle in which such animals as swimming moose and deer sometimes played a part.

I was splitting wood early one morning, and occasionally glancing at the debris-heavied swell of the flood, when I realized the throaty excitement of migrating birds was mixing headily with the seasonal noises. Vena came out about that time, her red apron white with flour, and together we hurried toward the open bank, Bushman following.

The sun was so bright among the islands downriver that, like Vena, I had to hold a palm against the gleam. Then we made out hundreds of trumpeting wild fowl moving through the sunrise in great smoky streaks.

"It isn't more geese, is it?" Vena asked.

"No, sandhill crane."

Odd thing, wilderness, I thought, watching the flight vanish upriver. The urge for it reached deep into the soul of man, mighty close to the steamy start of things. It was hard to realize that only a few weeks before I'd been in the city, hungering for this sort of life. Civilization now seemed a million light years away.

I didn't trust my voice to say very much just then, so, one hand in Bushman's collar, I put it as simply as I could.

"Are you happy, too?" I asked Vena.

"Oh, yes," she said.

12

But How Do You Live?

"But how do you live?" someone was always writing.

To the first friend who put that question to her, Vena answered, reasonably enough, "Pretty well, all in all."

What this particular inquirer and most of the others really meant, though, was: "How do you make a living?" Even such phrasing wouldn't have been intended as personally as it might have sounded. What the asker generally wondered was if he could also escape to such an apparently carefree existence and maintain himself in food, clothing, and the other necessities.

"Don't you find earning money a problem?" someone wrote that spring.

We did, certainly. On the other hand, we'd always found it a problem anywhere.

Here in the wilderness a lot of things were in our favor. Our lives themselves had become our entertainment, and we didn't have to spend money on shows and other amusements designed for a largely unamused multitude. Buying our food in large quantities was already helping keep costs down. Later we hoped to supplement our meals deliciously with wild fish and additional wild meat, with the output of Vena's small garden, and with the increasing amounts of wild fruits and vegetables that were free for the fun of gathering.

For us, writing seemed to be the answer. Now that our quarters were built, and Vena and Bushman and I could contemplate with some degree of satisfaction the food and firewood we'd laid by, I could no longer find any excuse for not getting at my typewriter steadily.

"Well, goodby, dear," I announced one morning. Bushman, crowding near, wagged his appreciation of my formalized kiss.

"Are you going somewhere?" Vena asked.

"To the office," I said. "I'll see you at lunch time. Have a pleasant morning."

I moved my small work table over by the windows, skittered a chair around, rolled a white sheet of paper into the portable typewriter, and made ready to engage in my profession.

Whatever else may be said about creative writing, it requires a certain amount of concentration. This had not bothered me before because I'd early been conditioned to the clamor and distractions of a newspaper office. I discovered now, however, that the quiet everyday casualnesses of a wife have considerably more impact than even the raucous interruptions of some acquaintance or associate which, because they do not personally involve you, don't crack the shell of your inner consciousness.

"What shall we have for dinner?" and "Can you see what Bushman is barking at?" were, I found, far more devastating to my line of thought than: "What did the mayor say about his nephew's getting that highway contract?"

It seemed natural for Vena to think aloud, and I considered it was lonely enough for her here without my shutting myself off from her world. So I tried to give her remarks the thought they merited without, at the same time, losing my tenuous connection with my own make-believe world. But finally the moment would come each day when I'd find myself reading the same uncompleted paragraph sometimes for the dozenth time.

"He's at the office," I eventually got in the habit of saying.

"I'm sorry," was usually the reply. "I forgot."

If, however, anything important was in balance, that was something else again. There could always be the equivalent of a telephone call or of even a hurried visit. All in all, it worked out exceedingly well. In fact, with the perseverence of my craft, I ultimately became so conditioned to Vena's usually being only a few feet from me that it was on the days when she was away, perhaps in town with Bushman for the mail, that I found it most difficult to keep my mind on the writing before me.

If I had ever been afraid that Vena would find herself with nothing to do mornings when I departed for my lone corner by the windows, I would have gravely underestimated her. She had a growing schedule of occupations and the time, finally, to become really engrossed in them.

These activities of Vena's were, in addition to the satisfaction they brought both of us, one more reason why we were living as well as we were. For time is money. When you go down to the store and buy a complete meal packaged in compartmented aluminum, you're buying not only the food but the time it took to prepare it. You are saving your own time, in other words, by purchasing the time of someone else.

Essentially, what we were buying by living in the wilderness was time—time which we hoped we could reallocate the way we wanted most. The real cost of anything is, of course, the amount of time you have to work to pay for it. For instance, you can either labor several hours at a job and then take the money and buy the family a dinner at a restaurant, or you can work just long enough to purchase the raw ingredients, then prepare the meal yourself, wherever you want.

"At least, I have one big advantage," Vena said one day when the stove was smoking. "I don't know anything about cooking to begin with."

I realized what she meant. Having been dancing professionally, producing stage shows, and traveling most of her life, she'd never had the opportunity to learn to cook. And from the little I knew myself about the subject, I appreciated that for anyone schooled in the modern laboratory of rotisseries, electric blending mechanisms, and thermostatically controlled heat all this would have been a long step backwards. Vena was having her troubles with the eccentricities and the waywardness of wood stoves. But, at least, she was starting at the beginning.

Fortunately, we both discovered that in the woods we liked what is thought of as good, plain food. Most of the time in Boston, meals had been, by and large, a nuisance and a begrudged necessity. But here, far from the humdrum tensions of city living, it was proving possible, as it had nowhere else, to enjoy the simple pleasures of life—browning frypan bread, steaming coffee, and sputtering bacon. The crackling of pine kindling in our small stove took on an unexpected cosiness, making our cabin seem all at once as snug and satisfying as a mansion.

Bread gave us the most trouble: *us* because you can't live in a one-room log cabin with someone you love and not become involved in those of her immediate problems that touch you both; *bread* because we ate it at nearly every meal and perhaps, too, because baking bread for the first time can get to be a problem anywhere.

We made out for awhile on the bannock—essentially flour, salt, baking powder, and water, cooked in an open frying pan—with which I was familiar from other trips into the outdoors.

"There's just one trouble," Vena said one evening when the sunset seemed to be floating in the river.

"What's that?"

"It still isn't bread," she said.

Sourdough bread proved to be the eventual solution. I knew nothing of this then. Neither did Vena, although she also remembered reading that it is the only breadstuff that will rise in any sort of log cabin condition short of freezing.

It was the coolness of our cabin, as a matter of fact, that was causing most of her difficulties. Having warm eiderdown sleeping robes, we found ourselves uncomfortable during any night warmer than 30° below zero if an overnight fire was burning.

Although Vena combatted this coolness by wrapping her sponges in coats and other warm coverings, the final loaves remained small, tough, and dense; not that Bushman and I minded too much. To me, bread seemed to be bread; and it was true enough, as I tried to point out, that the only ingredient lacking in the laboriously sliced slabs was air. As for Bushman, he welcomed the somewhat bonelike additions to his diet.

For a woman, though, I guess it was frustrating. In a way, Dudley Shaw didn't ease the psychological overtones of the situation. When he stopped in for lunch, when traveling this part of his trapline twice a week, he politely unwrapped his own two slices of bread. It was his contribution, he explained as diplomatically as he was able, bread being difficult to come by in the Far North.

"Well," Vena had to admit, "yes, it does seem to be that."

"Sourdough," Dudley said, "That's the answer. Noble concoction."

Dudley was kind enough to give us some fourteen-year-old sourings for a beginning.

"Just started nicely," he said.

Unfortunately, through our own ignorance—replenishing the sourings with leftover flapjacks and such and keeping them in a lard pail, both common if inadvisable practices—we eventually lost this venerable starter. However, another that Vena began remained potent and healthy.

One of the women in town told Vena how to go about it. I came into the cabin with an armful of kindling one afternoon, after she and Bushman had been to Hudson Hope for the mail, and I found her dissolving a newly purchased package of dry yeast in some water.

"Going to try yeast bread for a change?" I asked her.

"Not again," she said. "Everyone says the cabin is too cold. No, Edith McFarland was telling me how to start another sourdough sponge."

"You use a package of regular dry yeast?"

"Either that or a yeast cake," Vena said. "Oh, you can do it by mixing a cup apiece of plain flour and water and putting it in a warm place to sour. The trouble is, Edith says, there are over three thousand different wild yeasts, and you never know what sort of flavor or consistency you're going to end up with. That's why it's better to start growing your own yeast this way."

"Growing your own yeast?" I said.

"That's what the sourdough starter really is."

I began stacking the finely split spruce in the oven to dry. "You must have really gone into the subject."

"Just self-defense," she said, shoving a strand of hair up out of her eyes. "I feel such a fool, Brad. Any woman, if she wants to go to the trouble, should be able to cook such a common necessity as bread."

Something of what was passing through my mind must have showed on my face.

"It's all right, really," she laughed. "I don't mind. It's just that it makes me feel so useless, and I've never liked to feel useless."

"I didn't bring you to the woods just to work."

"At least, I feel as if I'm working for something important," Vena said, scraping the new starter into a scalded glass jar and covering it loosely. "Here, if something I cook doesn't come out right, I can't just throw up my hands and feel sorry for myself. I can't escape to a restaurant and forget all about it, either."

"There's always Bushman," I told her.

"No, not in the long run. Our food supplies won't stand much more of that. I can't run down to the store, either. No, I'm afraid you and I will have to eat most of my mistakes. What are you thinking now?"

Something about the way she asked it made me nervous.

"I was wondering if you minded all this too much, all the trouble and all the going without."

"Why, Brad." She swung around suddenly and confronted me, eyes bright and small chin set. "It's not like going without. It's, well, like building up your appetite until you can hardly wait. Then everything, once you do get it, is so delicious you can hardly stand it. As for the work, I wouldn't miss it for anything."

"Most of us could stand missing a lot of work."

"Don't you see?" It was almost as if she was gripping my arms to make me understand. "Back in Boston you didn't really need anything I could do around the house. Most of all, as far as making a home went, I didn't even feel necessary to myself."

She stopped.

"Maybe I'm not being very clear," she continued. "But I used to want to do useful things for us, only there wasn't really anything purposeful or essential to do. So I used to try to fill in with unnecessary tasks that didn't matter at all; running on special errands to the store for almost every meal, shining ornaments that might just as well have stayed hidden in a closet, going to parties that didn't mean a thing, fussing over inconsequentials—"

"A man gets a lot of that, too."

"I find that the more I do here, where it really matters to us," she went on, "the more there is I can do. Everything, I guess, sort of feeds on itself and is self-replenishing, whereas back in the city I could feel myself running dry."

"Maybe part of that is because you never did have much experience as a housewife," I said.

"Maybe," she said, "but I've talked to other women who've been housewives all their lives. And you'd be surprised to know how much the pattern is the same. Everything has been made so time-saving and comfortable in the city that women just don't feel indispensable any more."

"You're certainly not indispensable here," I said.

"At least I can try. And before I'm done, I'll be baking real bread, too. At least, I will if everyone keeps on helping me the way they have."

The way she said it made me feel even more uneasy. It was as if she was giving a lot too much importance to such a simple matter.

"Well, I guess I'd better be getting some work done myself," I said.

"You haven't finished today's pages yet?"

"Not yet," I said, and I couldn't understand why I should feel so guilty about something which must be routine.

The only way most writers I know can get any work accomplished is by following a schedule. However, there are different kinds of schedules. When I worked on newspapers and business publications, the constantly recurring deadlines kept me producing regularly. Now that I was on my own, I found that to accomplish anything I had to set a definite minimum of words to be written each and every day.

Without some such concrete goal, I discovered I could put in the working time and still get nothing done. But make my daily target, say, four pages, and

I'd get in the habit of worrying away at those pages in my mind until, sometimes just before turning in at night, I'd almost always get them done.

Besides, such a routine let me retain a sort of freedom, and a major reason Vena and I were here was in pursuit of freedom. If I wanted an outing, for example, I could free myself for it by doing the next day's pages in advance. Or, less satisfactorily, I could make them up afterwards.

Although Vena and I kept chores to a minimum, there were also a certain few things that had to be done each day to keep our secluded world functioning. No matter what the weather, for instance, we always needed wood, for we used it for cooking and for warming water as well as for heating the cabin. Then there was the maintaining of our water-bucket brigade. Lamps had to be filled, a task we prudently performed out of doors in all temperatures because of the fire danger.

Afternoons when I lingered late at the typewriter, I found myself waiting for the exact moment of dusk when it would be too dark to continue indoors without a light. That was the time of day I liked best for working outside. Whatever wind there was would hush, almost as if the world was holding its breath. A great peace would seem to rise about everything, and *rise* was the word, for night, I discovered in the wilderness, comes from the land itself rather than from the heavens.

A canyon, in reality an ancient and long-dry river channel a half mile above our cabin, had been a haven for a murky depth of darkness throughout the day. I explored this ravine sometimes, and it was also a sanctuary for owls who occasionally became suddenly moving masses, gliding ahead of me on whispering wings.

This canyon seemed throughout the mornings and afternoons to shelter what was left of the previous night. Then, as the sun sunk lower, it filled more and

more densely with the coming evening, until darkness
finally spilled over its dented brim and innundated the
encircling woods.

Shadows were continuing to darken over the land, as
Bushman and I walked slowly cabinward the second
evening after Vena's visit with Mrs. McFarland. Although blackness was so dense along the ground that I
could hardly see where to set my boots, the upper
branches of the poplars and birches were still softly
illuminated against the sky. I could see greyness ascending the hills that slanted above the flat on the
north. The tops of these were still brilliant with sunlight, and I saw two black shapes that must have been
moose emerging from the deepening gloom below and
climbing into the radiance.

The final addition of shadows which meant night
still had not been reckoned when we reached the outskirts of our clearing. Below in the river, the residue of
the departing day ran silver in the pools and coves.
Lamp light spreading out of the cabin windows made
me realize again how glad I always was to get back.

Warmness closed about me when, with Bushman
sliding ahead of me, I pushed into the cabin. The air,
which was brisk with the smell of the fire and of cooking, was somehow softer than it was outside. Vena was
busy over by the kitchen cabinet, and she had flour on
her red apron, which was too small to be as effective as
it was picturesque. There was flour on her face, too.

"Hello, darling," she said, and when she backhanded
a wisp of hair out of her eyes, some additional flour
was transferred to her forehead, giving her a pleasingly
domestic look. "I must have lost track of time. You
don't mind if we eat a little later than usual, do you?"

"No, I don't mind," I said. "Isn't that a mulligan I
smell on the back of the stove?"

"It isn't that nearly everything isn't ready," she said.
"But I thought that perhaps you wouldn't mind waiting
until my bread is out of the oven."

"Oh," I said, "that's what you've been doing?"

"You sound as if you think this won't be any good, either."

"No, I don't," I laughed. "You know I don't. I've never complained about your bread or anything else. If all I'd wanted was a cook, I could have hired one."

Then she was laughing, too, although in an odd way.

"I know," she said. "You've been wonderful that way. But I don't want to keep on stretching my luck. I'm trying one more time, just the way Dudley told me to."

There was nothing really difficult about making sourdough bread, Dudley Shaw had advised. Take your starter, he'd explained as carefully as he could. "Add enough flour and lukewarm water to make, say, about three cups of sponge. Let this stand in a warm location overnight or from six to eight hours, whereupon it should be bubbling and giving off an agreeable yeasty odor.

From here on, the general procedure remained the same. You took out, in the above instance, two cups of sponge. You placed the remainder aside. That comprised your next starter, Dudley had explained.

To these two cups of sponge, Vena said she had added four cups of flour, two tablespoons of sugar, one teaspoon of salt, and two tablespoons of shortening. She'd mixed the first three of these, then made a depression in their center. She blended the melted shortening and the sponge in the hollow. A soft dough had resulted. This she'd kneaded for about four minutes.

"And this time I didn't take any nonsense from it, either," she told me. "I think that's where I went wrong before."

"Keep attacking," I could still hear the old trapper cautioning, his eyes blinking amiably behind thick-lensed spectacles. "Don't gentle it. That's where most cheechakos make their mistake. Too much pushing and pressing lets the gas escape that's needed to raise the stuff. Just bang the dough together in a hurry, cut off loaves to fit your greased pans, and put them in a warm place to raise."

He had explained that the dough, once it had plumped out to double size, should be baked some fifty to sixty minutes in a moderately hot oven that, preferably, is warmest the first fifteen minutes. Baking should double the size of the loaves.

One tested "in the usual way," the old settler had added. He'd elucidated, probably because it had seemed necessary, that the "usual way" was to wait until the loaves seemed crisply brown, then to jab in a straw. If the bread was done, the straw would come out dry and at least as clean as it was when inserted.

I've felt ever since that dusk that about the only cooking odors that even approach the aroma of baking bread in the wilderness are the sizzling smell of good grilled bacon, coffee bubbling in the heat of a campfire, and fat venison sputtering over hardwood coals. By the time Vena drew the two plump brown loaves out of the oven and pronounced them done, I could hardly wait any longer.

"I made them longer and slimmer than usual," she said, "so there'd be more crust."

"They certainly look good," I told her. "Here, you'd better go outdoors, Bushman."

"He'll be all right," she said. "He's so used to eating my mistakes that he thinks this is for him."

"Well, it's not," I said, watching the knife saw through the crisp tan crust. "Lie down, Bushman. Go over there and lie down."

"I think it should have risen a little more," Vena said, examining a slice critically. "I won't be in such a hurry later on, but I didn't want to keep you waiting."

"It looks fine to me," I said. "Sourdough bread is supposed to be denser than the usual bakery loaves, isn't it? That's one reason it stays moist longer. Aren't we going to try it?"

"I'll put the mulligan on the table. We can help ourselves. I've some hot applesauce, too. Will that be enough, do you think?"

I thought it would be enough, and it was. The bread, nutty and substantial, really set off the meat and vegetables. I even had a final hot slice with the fruit. Vena, I noticed, reached for one, too.

"It is good," I said, resting a hand on her arm. I was relieved to have that crisis over and to have everything between us functioning evenly the way it had before. "That's another bugaboo you won't ever have to worry about again. Satisfied?"

"Not satisfied, exactly," she said softly, "but I feel a lot more complete."

13

Isn't Spring a Relief?

"I know it must be wet and muddy and all," one letter said. "But after all the snow and cold, isn't spring a wonderful relief?"

Well, it was wonderful, all right. But a relief? I couldn't remember, walking in fresh snow, and being startled by the explosive emergence of grouse from beneath a drift, and think that. Neither could I recall the almost inexpressible snugness of being indoors by the fire, with everything we wanted or needed nearby, and have any such sensations. Nor could I remember with such a stirring of pleasure the warm arrival of a chinook and feel that way.

The swiftly sinking swish of old snow preceded us now when we walked through parts of the wilderness where chinooks, spring, and the sun had not yet melted the drifts. It never ceased giving us an odd feeling to see and hear apparently solid crust rippling and settling just ahead of our crunching feet.

Mornings when we were outdoors in the first warm sunshine, poplar leaves snapped open like noisy popcorn.

"Here when spring comes," Vena said, "it doesn't fool around, does it?"

Yellow jackets happily buzzed flowering pussy willows. Cardinals, robins, and the scouts of the coming cliff swallows added to the general excitement. Tiny blue moths brushed us. The ground smelled earthy and good.

Across the river, a mist of the lightest of greens began clinging so delicately to the tops of the tall poplars that it was only in the first morning light that it could be distinguished. This green became denser and deeper, like an engulfing wave, until the day arrived when we could no longer see the ground beneath or even the individual branches.

It was that way everywhere. Verdancy sprang up underfoot and stretched down from above. No longer did we enjoy the wonderful openness through which the gaze could roam unimpeded. The thickness was not like that of New England and Southeastern Canada where, more than once, I'd had to get down and crawl to make my way through spruce and alder. Here, except where there was the downfall that followed a fire, one could ride a horse nearly anywhere. But Vena and I, at least, preferring the open places, now seemed somehow shut in by the almost overpowering vegetation.

Spring a relief? No, in a way we found ourselves missing the openness of winter. King Gething, to whom we talked at Hudson Hope one mail day, sympathized with us.

Neil Gething, the sturdy, white-haired father of the family and the mining expert who had been a prime mover behind the present development of Hudson Hope coal mining properties, was explaining to Vena about some local wild edibles new to her. King and I were conversing at one corner of the long table in the sunny Gething kitchen.

"You'll have to come up to my mine later on," King was saying. "The road is out now, but later on I'll drive down and pick up the two of you. That's one way of beating the season."

"Beating the season?" I repeated.

"That's right," King replied, as he arranged cups on the table and started toward the stove. "You know, of course, that as far as vegetation is involved, every thousand feet you gain in elevation is the same as traveling six hundred miles further north. And six hundred miles north from here would put you up by Great Bear Lake in the Northwest Territories, not far from the Arctic Ocean. It's not nearly as thick now up at my diggings as it is down here at the Hope."

"We were thinking of riding up to Chinaman Lake for much the same reason," I told him. "Joe Barkley just asked us over to Beryl Prairie. Gene Boring said we could use a couple of his saddle horses, and Joe says they're ranging up by his place and that he'd put them in his corral for us."

"It'd be like going backward in time," King said, returning with a white teapot. "It'll still be winter partway up the slopes of the Butler Range there at Chinaman. On flat land, as you know, Spring moves northward something like fifteen miles a day. When it comes to a mountain, though, it only climbs about two hundred yards a week."

Our trip to the lake was delayed because the next day I got us some meat. It was a young black bear, and I came upon it while still hunting above the cabin at Box Canyon. Black bear were legal in British Columbia the year around. I'd been watching the tracks of this one for the past week, where he had been coming down from the kinnikinic-greened hills above Bull Creek through deadfall and the dry canyon to the river.

The emotions that quickened my breathing, I found when I got to work translating the young bruin into roasts and a rug, were different from those common to an ordinary hunt. Those were, in spite of the dinners and trophies that awaited success, largely sporting answers to an instinctive urge. This, I now discovered, was the direct reply to the demands of survival itself. This was for real.

Bushman, who'd been kept inside the cabin since he howled when left tied outside while I went hunting, was puzzled by the scent coming from my snow-scoured hands and from my bulging packsack. He kept backing away and stretching out his nose. Then his tail started flailing.

Vena, whose array of pots and kettles showed she had also been busy, was even more impressed. There was also a difference, I realized now, between being called upon to cook game meat in the city where there are butcher shops on every side and being provided with the same thing in the storeless wilderness.

The bear liver we had that evening was delicious, but no more so than Vena's dessert of highbush cranberries and rose hips.

"They were dry for being on the bushes all winter," she said, "but I just used more water. The liver's wonderful. It tastes just like calf's liver, doesn't it?"

"Yes," I said. "So is this wonderful."

She seemed pleased. I know I was. Even if we were no longer drawing down the money that our respective professions brought in cities, we were proving that we could still make out.

The rose hips had the flavor of fresh apples. The elusive sweetish sourness of the highbush cranberries furnished a provocative addition.

"We've even free vitamins," I said.

"We have?" she asked.

I'd been reading in one of the books which we'd started receiving regularly from the Open Shelf of the Public Library Commission in Victoria, which even paid postage both ways, that the juice of wild rose hips is from six to twenty-four times richer in Vitamin C than orange juice. Studies had found the scurvy-preventing vitamin in the raw pulp running from four thousand to nearly seven thousand milligrams per pound. Daily human requirements, to cite a yardstick, are estimated to be from sixty to seventy-five milligrams.

The aroma of roast bear that filled the cabin the next afternoon really started our taste buds tingling. Many individuals, the large majority of whom have never tasted bear meat nor smelled it cooking, are prejudiced against blackies and grizzly for one reason and another. One complaint often heard arises from the animal's eating habits. Yet the most ravenous bear is a finicky diner when compared to such delicacies as lobster and chicken.

It's true enough that not even a plump young yearling furnishes really good steaks, which is where many culinary attempts end. The meat is too fibrous. But even an oldster big enough to carpet a cabin will cook into roasts so moist and savory that you have to eat them to believe them. The meat then so resembles top grade beef that you can serve it as such to individuals who have vowed never to touch bear and actually have them back for second and third helpings.

And the stews such as the one we had on the day following? Well, if bear weren't such good eating, I'd have given up all thoughts of hunting them now that we had our rug.

Before we left on our trip to Chinaman Lake, we put up the remainder of the meat. It was a simple enough task. I cut the red flesh into lengths about the size of my forearm, following the membranous portions among the muscles as well as I could. The meaty bones, tastiest part of any game, Vena fitted into a kettle for mulligan. We saved out a couple of roasts, too, storing them inside a wooden box in a snow-filled cave near the cabin.

We stripped what we could of the membrane from the rest of the meat. Then we rolled the chunks in a thickly clinging mixture that we readied by stirring together three pounds of table salt, four tablespoons of allspice, and five tablespoons of black pepper.

I made spike holes in the shorter pieces, worked cord through them, and then tied them to a wire angled across the inside of our cache beyond the reach of small animals. I spread some old papers beneath to keep the drippings off the floor, wedged door and windows far enough ajar to maintain a circulation of cool air, and wondered if we could wait an entire month before sampling the results of our first experiment in curing our own meat.

"Are you going to send the hide out to be made up?" Vena asked. "It would feel nice underfoot on cool mornings, and I guess Bushman could find a use for it nights."

"Let's try sun-tanning it ourselves," I suggested.

Driving small nails about an inch apart, I tacked the hide with its fur against the outer southern wall of the cache where, protected by the wide eaves, it could cure in the sun. A pair of grey Canada jays at once volunteered their assistance, swooping low to peck at the red evidences of flesh that I hadn't scraped entirely away.

"Now why don't we see what else the wilderness has to offer?" I said. "Then I really have to settle down to writing. If we're going to make a real go of all this, I've got to begin earning some money."

"You still haven't made any sales?"

"Not one."

"Of course," she said, "it hasn't been very long."

"I know, but there hasn't even been a nibble."

She gazed upriver for a moment.

"What are your stories about? You haven't let me read any of them."

"Oh," I said, "the usual thing. Boy meets girl, boy loves girl, boy loses girl, boy gets girl."

"Aren't there an awful lot of those?"

"I suppose so. But there always have been."

"I mean," Vena said, "there must be hundreds of thousands of people who have been yearning all their lives to have a try at living the way you and I are now. Only they've never had the chance to do anything but dream. Beginning when we get back from Chinaman Lake, why don't you tell them what it is really like?"

The next morning when we struck off roughly northwest by compass through the woods toward Beryl Prairie and Joe and Clara Barkley's, it was as though no one had ever gone that way before. As far as that particular route was concerned, probably no human being had ever preceded us, although there were occasional game trails that we followed from time to time.

There's something about traveling along a game trail deep in the wilderness that brings an odd sense of relaxation, perhaps because others have tested that particular way before and found it good. There is the fact, too, that along such forest routes you have to pay less attention to where you're setting your feet and can, therefore, give more heed to what's going on all about: the sweep of an eagle, the concern of a doe with her straying fawn, and the rustling scurry of a chipmunk alert again after the drowsiness of winter.

When these short stretches ended, as they all soon did, it was still easy traveling through the tall poplars and slender lodgepole pine. A sense of anticipation, both an atavistic awareness of our primitive surroundings and the realization that a new experience lay ahead, whetted our nerve ends to an exquisite sensitivity.

"I think I know now how many of the pioneers' wives, the ones who loved what they were doing, must have felt back in Daniel Boone's day," Vena said now, and I noticed she kept her voice low.

"How's that?" I asked.

"Really alive," she said.

Spring, though, seemed as far advanced as it was

about the cabin, even when Bullhead became a snow-smoothed rotundity over our left shoulders. It wasn't until the next morning, after we had spent the night with our company-hungry friends and they'd started us off on Boring's two horses, that we began to catch up with the departing winter.

"How does it feel to be riding?" I asked Vena.

"Good," she said, sitting straight and very pretty in the saddle. "I'm not very sure of myself, though."

Bushman ran ahead, behind, and around, as if he'd been used to horses all his life. I was afraid at first that he'd make the two nervous, but after a few sniffs they paid him little attention.

"Joe said that Cloud is just about the gentlest gelding he ever saw."

"I guess he probably is," she said, "but I've never done much riding. Oh, some of us occasionally used to find a stable Sundays wherever we happened to be. I've never been off a bridle path before, though, and I've certainly never been in a western saddle."

"I've never ridden much, either," I said. "When I have, it's been either bareback or on English saddles. I guess we'd both better take it easy at first."

"That sorrel, Chinook, is a beauty."

"Yes, she is," I said. "She seems to have a head of her own, though. But Joe said she'll be all right as long as Cloud is with us."

"If we like them," Vena said, "do you suppose we may be able to buy them later on?"

"I don't see why not."

"It would be nice to have horses of our own," she said, holding the reins in one hand while she buttoned her jacket with the other. "I'd like to spend a lot of time with them, and really learn about them, and how to ride, and all."

More and more, bare trees were impressing the starkness of their branches against the blue sky, although behind and below us the glare of the river was softened by a green sea of leaves.

The bare hoofs of Chinook and Cloud crunched through a patch of muskeg brittle with ice. The ground was generally naked and brown, and what drifts there were bunched thicker and higher. The ascent became steeper. Bushman swiftly circled the remains of a log shack north of the trail. Then we, too, reached the top of the ridge. Ahead was the flat, white expanse of Chinaman Lake.

"Why," Vena said, "it's frozen."

A gaunt cabin, bare except for stove and bunks, was below in a tiny flat at the northern outlet of the small lake. We picketed the horses near it, where grass was greening among the residues of drafts, and unsaddled them.

"Do you want me to start a fire in the stove?" I asked.

Wind, from the glistening peaks of the Butler Range that stretched in a silent wall above the forested western side of the lake, was brisk in our faces. Snowbanks were vaporizing in the heat of the sun, and there was a warm earthy pungency to the preponderantly brown slopes.

"Oh, no, let's have a campfire," Vena said." "I've been looking forward to one. Let's not go indoors at all. Let's sleep out, too."

"All right," I said, and I felt myself smiling back at her.

I had been hoping to do just that, but then I hadn't known there would be a cabin.

That afternoon we cut long, dry poles with the ax which, with light eiderdowns and part of our nested cooking outfit and a few personal belongings, was all we had brought. With these light lengths of spruce for insurance, we set out to explore the ice which, we found, was solid enough in the middle of the lake but was candling in the shallow stretches near the outlet.

Wolf tracks, like those of huge dogs, were all about, and along one part of the northern shore, where for a small area the snow was packed as hard as the surface of a skating rink, there were the fresh skeletons of two moose, bones picked clean.

"Do they ever attack human beings?" Vena asked.

"Only in stories," I said.

We heard wolves howling across the lake the second evening while pine kindling was snapping and a nearby hump of snow was starting to steam in the hot breath of the flames.

"They don't sound terrible at all, do they?" Vena said, clasping her hands around her knees and staring over the campfire at the empty expanse of lake beyond. "They just sort of seem to belong with the freeness of all this."

"You didn't think that the first time you heard them," I said, "that first night up at our cabin site."

"I wasn't sure," she said. "Most of all, I guess, I wasn't sure of myself."

"You are now?"

"At least," she said, "I'm no longer afraid of every little thing. It's still a little difficult for me to realize why, but somehow I feel a lot safer sitting here beside a fire in the wilderness than I did a lot of nights back in Boston when you and I went walking in the Esplanade. Somehow, even when I try to analyze it, I really believe it is a whole lot safer here."

"The thing that makes it so hard to realize, I guess, is that man himself is the most vicious animal ever to walk the face of the globe. The terrible problems of the world are not between man and nature. They're between men and man."

"Nature is fine, isn't it?" she nodded. "The wrongs really are among human beings."

We had rabbit that night, cut into halves and slowly broiled on forked sticks over the coals. Five of the snares I'd set the night before held their prizes, so even

Bushman had more than his fill. The only trouble with varying hare, ordinarily, is its lack of fat, but we made up for that by roasting some of the leg bones from the fresh moose skeletons we'd discovered. Their rich marrow, secured by cracking the bones with a rock, was delicious.

Vena had gathered some fern fronds we'd carefully identified. These, cleaned of their papery husks and briefly boiled, had a delicately elusive taste that ranged between that of young asparagus and the tenderest of string beans. For dessert we had a boiled mixture of rose hips, kinnikinic berries, and highbush cranberries.

"Do you know," I said suddenly, "this trip alone should make an article for one of the outdoor magazines."

"All you've got to do is bring your writing to the woods, too," Vena nodded. "Why, there must be millions who'd be interested in knowing about living off the country."

"Living off the country," I repeated. "I'd like to write a book about that someday."

"The way the world is racing itself to build more and more destructive weapons," she said, "for a lot of people a book like that might mean the difference some day between surviving and starving to death."

"I suppose so," I said. "Here it all seems so far away. We listen on the radio to a dozen things that are wrong. But all we have to do is look around to see a thousand things that are right."

The wolves started howling again sometime during the night. Stars were bright overhead, and only wind-stirred coals remained of what had been a roaring fire. The browse bed, laboriously thatched with dozens of spruce boughs, was springy beneath me as I stirred, careful not to disturb Vena who was breathing serenely at my side. The big rangy creatures sounded as if they must be on the very outskirts of our small camp.

I had a few moment's doubt and then was embarrassed by it. The two picketed horses, silhouetted against the snow, were not even lifting their ears at the din. Then I had a sudden fear for Bushman's safety, but he was curled drowsily within my reach. His nose found my hand when I patted him, and then he lay back again.

The wild cacophony so engulfed the silence that I knew I couldn't ever get back to sleep, if only because of the sheer excitement of it. The next thing I knew I was startled by warmth burning red hot through my eyelids. It took me a minute to realize it was the morning sun.

"Hello." Vena was up on one elbow, smiling at me.

"Hello," I said.

"I thought you'd never wake up. You looked so comfortable I hated to disturb you. Isn't it peaceful here?"

"Did you hear the wolves last night?"

"Just before we went to bed, you mean? I don't know when I've ever slept so well. I suppose we really have to go back today, don't we? But I hate to leave. Why are you smiling at me like that?"

"A friend told me once," I said, "that there are two targets to point for in life: first, to get what you want, and, after that, to be able to enjoy it. Only the most fortunate, he said, achieve the second."

14

A Ride in the Woods

"What would I ever find to do?" one of Vena's friends wrote her. "Oh, I know, there's cooking, housekeeping, and all that. When your work is done, though, what do you do for relaxation? Here in Boston I can always go to a movie. Then there are the plays that are forever coming to town, often, as you well know, even before they reach New York. There are the lectures, the museums, and all the sporting events, both amateur and professional. There's bridge, and when you get tired of playing, you can always sit around and talk.

"Up North, though, you can't even have many people for friends. Didn't you say that the town is five or six miles away, with only one neighbor in between? And TV? That certainly must be out of the question. Why, you're even so far from everything that I don't imagine you can get very good radio reception."

Vena's voice ended on an up-note. She looked up from the letter she had been reading aloud, one of the small bundle that Bushman and I had just brought from Hudson Hope.

"You know," Vena said, "I haven't thought of it lately, but she's almost right. Except for the occasional movie King Gething screens in Hudson Hope, and except for her mistake about the radio, that letter is pretty accurate."

"Do you miss all those things?"

"I don't know," she said. Then she laughed. "I didn't until I started thinking about it, that's for sure."

"Isn't that just the point?"

"What do you mean?"

"She thinks we're bored."

"Bored?" Vena said, and the corners of her lips curled upward.

I waited for her to go on, but she stopped. I thought of the brief periods everyone goes through when nothing appears interesting and when every next motion seems to be too much of a futile effort. Then it doesn't make much difference where you are, except that I'd found myself at loose ends in cities far more often than I ever had in the wilderness. Here there were just too many interesting things—interesting in many cases because they directly affected our very existence.

"You are happier here as time goes on, aren't you?" I asked Vena now.

"Oh, yes," she said. "From that day when we went out finding wild foods I've liked it. That's something I'll remember always, no matter where we live. But I was never bored."

"You didn't really care for it before, though?"

"You know I don't mean that," she said. "I've always liked it far more than I ever dreamed I could. But, before, I was mostly an onlooker. When I started helping get our food it was as if I suddenly became a part of everything."

After the lake trip, spring seemed to move rapidly into summer. The river's constant roar filled the air, and the objects that floated into view captured more and more of our interest. We saw a lynx cross below the cabin and emerge safely, mostly legs now that its fur was flattened. Bank beaver were common. We watched dog-paddling black bear. There were a few deer. The best swimmers among the large animals, though, were the moose. We saw a cow moose one morning, her body high in the water, swimming backwards down the rapids in such a way that the torrent pressed a little tan calf protectively against her black bulk.

With the warming of the weather that was coincident with the rising of the water and the ridding of the river of ice, mosquitoes emerged in humming legions. A few had made their appearance earlier. These, however, had been big, hulking insects whose lethargic deliberateness had made it easy to dispose of them while they were still making up their minds. Incidentally, as a whole the insects were nowhere nearly as pestiferous as those I'd known in the East, at Moosehead Lake in Maine, for example, and along the salmon streams of Eastern Canada.

Tiny, busy mosquitoes appeared abruptly the first of June. They were not at all troublesome near the river, though, where there was a constant breeze. Although those almost invisible winged biters sometimes known as no-seeums prevailed at dusk and again at dawn, they never stayed out for long, and there were none of the little black flies that had been so annoying other places I'd been.

A manufacturer supplied us with a flask of diethyl toluamide, later the basis of several of the more effective commercial insect repellents. This usually kept mosquitoes so far away that they seldom made that first experimental landing and, as a matter of fact, generally didn't even remain close enough to whine about our ears. The liquid made available to us for testing was the pure product, to be diluted with alcohol. The most effective combination we found was three parts to one part of alcohol.

One of the reasons we seldom had to ask ourselves what there was to do was that we had made an arrangement, with a tentative option to buy, to use

Chinook and Cloud, the two horses we had ridden to Chinaman Lake. We picked up saddles, bridles, and other necessary gear mostly secondhand, and the total cost was very small. A big comfortable western saddle that had been given Ted Boynton by a dude, and which had been custom-made and expensive when new, cost me twenty dollars, for example.

I'd seldom seen Vena as pleased as she was now that she had a horse all her own. She used to go out every half-hour at first to make sure that Cloud was not tangled in his picket rope or that he had not eaten all the greenery within reach. By tethering the horses with long ropes tied with a non-jamming and non-tightening bowline knot to a leg just above above the hoof, we arranged for them to stay fat by living off the country.

"If we buy them, what will we do this fall when there's no more graze?" Vena wanted to know.

"If we think there's some chance we may be back in this country again," I said slowly, "we can just turn them loose if you want. That's the way most of the saddle horses here winter. They keep in good shape on peavine, vetch, and other food that's in the swamps and on the hillsides."

"That way we couldn't ride them this winter, could we?"

"We'd have to buy bundles of oats and feed them if we kept them in for riding."

"That's what I'd like to do this winter," she said, "if it wouldn't cost too much."

"Feed prices vary. I was talking to Matt Boe, though, and he said he could deliver good big bundles here for seven and a half cents apiece. If we give each horse one in the morning and another at dusk, he said, they'll keep in good shape the little we'll be using them. So it'll only cost us thirty cents a day to keep in both horses."

"Oh, can we?"

"Sure," I said. "Sure, it'll be fun. We'll need a corral, though."

We might as well enjoy Chinook and Cloud to the utmost while we could, I thought. Then we could always sell them and the gear for just about what we'd paid for everything. We could if we wanted to, that is.

But even though it would probably be only sensible to get rid of the saddles and other equipment rather than let age and chipmunks whittle away at them, I thought that Vena might prefer, too, to know that our horses could still go on roaming the hills the year round, for all practical purposes free.

I'd already spoken of this vaguely to Joe Barkley. He said that inasmuch as the two were already accustomed to ranging at Beryl Prairie, if Vena and I turned them loose there, they'd be unlikely to leave. This was particularly true, Joe added, because a local abundance of peavine and vetch provided the best grazing hereabouts. They'd join the bunch of horses already there, Joe said. He'd keep an eye on them when they all occasionally came around his place for salt, although he said that Chinook and the rest of the horses hereabouts, unlike most of the horses I'd seen other places, were accustomed to taking care of themselves.

Even when the clamor and confusion of the metropolis were pressing around me again, more stiflingly than ever because of the contrast of this freedom I was now enjoying, it would be good to think of our horses, at least, remaining living parts of the dream.

"You seem so far away," Vena was saying. "What's that about a corral?"

"It shouldn't take long to throw one up. Let's have a look around. The easiest way to build it, I guess, will be with posts and poles."

"How about that barbwire you found last winter in that old cabin we're using for our cache?"

"That'll be just the thing, too," I said.

The simplest thing would have been to put up the enclosure so it would have included a portion of the creek. But the difficulty was that this was our water supply. With our cabin built near where the brook plunged into the Peace, there was no easy way to let water run through the corral the year around and still keep our own source pure.

So we selected a flat open stretch of land down wind of the cabin and worked on the corral at odd hours. In a week the job was finished. Turned loose in it, the horses investigated it throughly, kicking up their heels while Bushman barked. Then they began nipping the choice tips of False Solomon Seals.

Riding the first few times made us stiff and sore, and there were areas where it removed patches of skin, too.

"My knees feel it most," Vena said.

"So do mine, but they'll get toughened."

"I suppose it's the saddle," she said. "I have to use my knees so much, along with my ankles, to take up the shock and to keep from bouncing."

"We'll get used to that," I said, "I'm not worried about that at all."

"Then there are the places where I don't have any skin left," Vena said, "like on the insides of both knees."

"It'll all work out," I said, "when we get the rhythm of it. That's it, I suppose, the rhythm."

"I don't know about Chinook," Vena said, "but Cloud has a lot of different rhythms, and when he isn't on a trail, he adds a few more. It's not just a matter of keeping time. It's keeping time the right way. I wish someone was around who could really teach us how to ride correctly."

"I don't think they know themselves what they do," I said. "They just grew up riding, and they never thought much of anything about it, just as we never thought about walking. We just tried, I suppose, and kept on trying until we were getting around."

"I suppose so, but that doesn't help much now."

"There may be a way," I told her. "King Gething told me that the best way to learn to ride naturally is to go on a several-day trip. By the time you're through, he said, you've learned in self-defense to stop irritating the sore spots you shouldn't have been irritating, anyway."

"Why don't we do it?"

"All right," I said. "Now that I've sent off that article on wild foods and the Chinaman Lake trip, let's accept King's invitation and ride up to his mine and back. It's not too rough cross-country, he says, and we'll come up against a lot of different kinds of terrain. Then we can get in some extra riding while we're staying there."

She didn't say anything for a moment. Then she smiled.

"When do we leave?" she asked.

"How about the day after tomorrow? There's something I want to do first."

"Where are you going now?"

"Riding," I said. "I'd like to go alone this one time if you don't mind. And would you keep Bushman in, please?"

"You'll be all right?" she asked.

"If I can't handle Chinook when Cloud isn't along," I said, "it's time I was finding out."

Chinook was docile enough when I saddled her, although, as usual, she danced some while I was tightening the latigo and trying to get the bit past her teeth. She kept jerking her head toward Cloud while I was untying the halter shank, coiling it, and fastening it with a rawhide lace to the front of the saddle. Then when I got the reins in my left hand and the saddle horn in my right, with my back to her head and my left foot awkwardly in the stirrup, she started before I was ready.

"Whoa," I was saying, "whoa."

It was all right, though, because the forward impetus swung me into the seat. Then my off toe was groping for the iron stirrup which kept banging me on the ankle, and I was trying to turn her and to keep her balance, all at the same time. Cloud was whinnying. When Chinook crooked her neck to answer, I managed to keep her head turned until she was going in the direction I wanted.

She had her mind made up that she was travelling to town and that, in any event, if she had to leave Cloud behind, she certainly wasn't going into the woods and upriver. By digging my heels into her ribs, I finally got her up past the cabin. Vena waved, and I heard her telling Bushman to be quiet. Then we reached a loop of Bull Creek that Chinook decided she wasn't going to cross.

"How's about a drink?" I said, as if we were both in this thing together, and I wanted to be agreeable about everything. "Go ahead and have a drink."

I loosened the reins. She ducked her head several times, but the creek bed here was steep and narrow. She tried bending her front legs. She gave this up, though, when her bare hoofs slipped. Then she wanted to go back.

I turned her three or four times, bringing her again to the creek. She wouldn't cross it, although the water was no more than three feet wide, and the whole terrain was perfectly safe. When I went back the trail a ways and then ran her for it, she reared at the last moment and stood there quivering.

There didn't seem to be any use in having a horse and not being able to manage her. The trouble, of course, was that I wasn't sure of myself and that I didn't know anything about riding. Well, I decided, it was about time I learned what I could. Settling myself as solidly as possible, I reached up and broke off a poplar branch.

Just the motion set Chinook off, and she was across the brook in a single leap. The impetus shoved me hard against the stirrups, then slammed me into the cantle. I was thinking how she'd be reassured, now that she'd found I'd been right and that there was nothing at all to the crossing. Then I was just thinking about how to stay on.

Chinook was running through the woods. Whenever an obstruction such as a log appeared in the way, she leaped it. Every few steps, she bucked. If she had twisted at all, I would have been off after the first lunge or two. As it was, whenever I left the saddle, I always found it there to receive me again.

I was hammering against the leather so hard that my neck ached. At first, I clung to Chinook with my thighs and knees while managing to keep enough spring in them and my ankles to take up some of the shock. Trees bruised my legs. I kept turning and ducking in an effort not to be swept off. Then I realized that the strength was leaving my leg muscles. The pain knifing down from my hips to my shins didn't bother me too much because I didn't have time to think about it. But when all the tension left my legs, leaving them limp, all I could do was grab for the saddle horn and hold on with all my might.

It was then that I learned something about balance. My body must have been equalizing itself automatically, for now that I was gripping the horn I was no longer an instinctively centering weight but, instead, a loosening sack attached to a peg. I tried to hold myself down in the saddle. Young poplars were slashing across me. A black stump loomed up in their midst. Chinook veered, and suddenly there was no longer anything beneath me but atmosphere.

I was yelling something. Then I was on my back in a patch of bunchberries. It wasn't any worse than being tackled hard in football, only I wondered why I wasn't just relaxing there instead of shouting and scrambling up. Then I realized that I was yelling, "Whoa!"

Chinook was standing there, the two black reins trailing on the ground in front of her. She was breathing hard, and when she backed away from me and stepped on a rein, the resulting tug caused her to rear.

"Easy," I said, forcing my voice low and keeping my motions gradual. I didn't want her galloping back to the cabin riderless and frightening Vena. For that matter, maybe she wouldn't even stop at the cabin; and saddled and bridled, she could get hung up somewhere. "Easy, now. Whoa."

Then my foot was on a rein. When she jerked back again, the tightening leather fairly straightened into my hand. I've wondered afterward why I tried it again, alone out there in the woods. I suppose if I hadn't been alone, though, I wouldn't have had the temerity to risk making a spectacle of myself, although what I did seemed to be the only thing there was to do.

The second time was infinitely worse. My legs gave out sooner, not that the pain made much difference any more, but I couldn't make them grip or take up any of the jar. I bounced so high against the thumping saddle that it was difficult to maintain my seat.

I had very little control over my body any longer, and I had far less over Chinook. It wasn't that she was a bad horse in any sense, for she could have easily wiped me off by going under a low limb, while if she had put any twists in her straightforward bucking, I wouldn't have lasted a minute. It was more as if she'd been accustomed to being on her own and making her own decisions, and now she'd worked herself into such a state that she couldn't quit any more than I could.

She was running now through an old burn, and I could see the short, charred ends of poplar saplings like spears below me. That was when I grabbed leather again. The realization came to me, too, that she was pounding along the edge of the cliff which, with the way the river kept undermining the shale, was treacherous at best.

I pulled on both reins, then sawed on them, all without effect. Finally, I concentrated on one rein and eventually got her neck twisted so far that she began veering in a wide circle. That was something, at least, although her wildly plunging pace didn't slacken. When I tried to halt her by steering her into a great fallen spruce, fearful all the while of the crash that might result, she just disregarded the direction in which her head was being hauled.

What halted her finally, I don't know. I suppose the fact that I'd fortunately secured a stout bridle enabled me to tire out her neck muscles. She began turning in such a tight circle that she could no longer run, although when I thought I had her at enough of a standstill so I could descend safely, she gave a final pitch that sent me sprawling. This time, however, I kept hold of the reins.

My aching legs were trembling, but I noticed that she was quivering, too. Her heaving body was so white with sweat in places that despite everything I was sorry for her. But it was no time to think of that.

This time when I got into the saddle, I grasped the cheek of the bridle as firmly as I could and somehow found my right stirrup in a single, shaky motion. Then I tried to forget about Chinook's mouth as I held her head as high as I could. She didn't seem to be able to get started running again, and each time she tried to pitch, I tugged her head higher.

Then, grimly, I turned her back the way we'd come. She balked once more at the creek, and then she wanted to leap it, but partly because I was afraid I would never survive another plunge, I made her walk across. Then I turned her and walked her back. I walked her back and forth through the water until she was doing it automatically.

Then, not relaxing the pressure of my left hand on the reins, I broke off another poplar branch. Scarcely daring not to leave well enough alone, I waved it back and forth by her head. Nothing happened. I brought it down against her flank the way I'd meant to that first time. Muscles twitched, but the only other effect was that she obediently picked up her pace. I took her back and forth across the stream again, and then, hot and exhausted, I headed her home.

Cloud whinnied as we approached, but Chinook gave no heed. She stood, head down, while I tied her halter, then pulled off bridle, saddle, and saddle blanket. She was so wet that on second thought, although I was sore and shaken enough not to feel much like it, I got an old piece of blanket and a brush and rubbed her until she was glossy. She just stood there, never moving while I worked all around her.

When I was finished, I stroked her gleaming neck. She turned her velvet nose and, to my surprise, softly nuzzled me.

"Did you have a good ride?" Vena asked when I went in.

"Yes, it was quite a ride."

She was looking at me with an intent expression, but I guess she could see I didn't want to talk about it, for she turned back to the stockings she was darning. She must have been worried, I thought, because it usually took some sort of cataclysmic occurrence before she could get herself to do any darning.

"I had an idea you might be back early," she said. "It looks so much like rain."

It wasn't that I made a practice of keeping anything from her. It was just that I didn't want her to worry. She didn't say any more about it, although just from the condition of my legs, which were raw in places and which were stuck to my trousers, she could certainly tell that something had happened.

Then I realized that she'd concern herself needlessly

if I kept silent, and that this worry would spread to other things that she'd become afraid I might be concealing from her if only for her own peace of mind. I told her then, and it didn't seem important any more.

"It might be just as well if you ride only Cloud for awhile," I said. "Not that I think I'm any better rider than you, but I just don't want you getting hurt."

"I don't want you getting hurt, either," she said, "especially not alone out in the woods somewhere."

"I think Chinook and I understand each other now," I said. "I don't think she'll ever be any more trouble."

"I hope not," Vena said, putting down her work and coming toward me. "I think maybe it's easy for me to understand Chinook a little bit, too."

15

Suddenly It's Summer

Rain did begin falling soon after we'd started our ride up what were the lower slopes of Bullhead Mountain toward King Gething's coal mine. The croaking of frogs in the mossy canyons behind us had been harsh and coarse like an ungreased farm wagon jolting and thumping over a rocky road. Now that the drops started to pelt down, it lifted and sharpened in timbre.

The two light sleeping bags we were carrying, plus a small amount of extra clothing and some personal belongings, were wrapped in waterproof tarpaulins and tied behind our saddles. The rain could not harm anything. The horses, arching their necks, even seemed to like it. As for Bushman, he was so overjoyed at the prospect of going somewhere, anywhere, that he was oblivious to everything but the excitement of the moment.

Sunlight came out ahead. The horses started to gallop. The sparsely falling drops became, in the sudden radiance, a barrier of platinum cords through which we forced ourselves as effortlessly as in a dream.

"Isn't it beautiful?" Vena said.

"I thought you didn't like rain?"

"I don't like rain when there's traffic to splash me, and gutters to step in over my shoes, and taxis to wait for."

"I hadn't thought of it like that," I said. "I guess I feel the same way."

"I don't like winter in the city, as far as that goes," Vena said, "but it's magnificent here. For that matter, I don't like spring there, either. It just gets you worked up, and then nothing happens except summer."

"How about summer? Of course, here in the wilderness you've only seen a few days of it."

"That's strange," she said after a moment. "But I think I like summer better there. Do you know why?"

"Because it used to mean vacation time?"

"The feeling probably started with that, I suppose. Then, later on, there were the summer theatres and the other means of getting away. I guess that was it, the contrast." She drew a deep breath. "Here, without that kind of contrast, summer just sort of closes in about you."

I nodded.

"I haven't seen autumn yet, of course," she went on, "but from what I hear it must be exciting. No, I guess I like summer in the woods the least of all seasons. Is that a creek ahead there?"

A silvery pool confronted us. I had never come across it before, and now I saw it was apparently the source of the tiny brook I'd seen while scouting above Box Canyon and which seeped back into the ground before reaching the surface of the river.

Breezes curved lines across the water whose harmonious designs were complicated by the pearl-like indentations of raindrops and by the brighter splashes of water that had accumulated on overhanging trees. As we looked, a gust sighed through the leaves of these birches so noisily that the sound drowned out even the increasing plop and blob of whorl-fashioning drops.

Secluded as it was, the still somehow tranquil spot was apparently a favorite drinking place. We saw the fresh tracks of moose, bear, deer, and smaller forest folk. Chinook and Cloud wanted drinks, too, and we waited while they lowered their heads.

Ahead, a gentle but persistent slope slanted upward to the level though which, some two miles inland, King Gething's road led from the portage to his mine. We climbed on foot, leading the horses and pausing occasionally to rest and to look. The Peace River opened behind· us. Although we could not see the cabin because of the forest, we made out the kinnikinic-lush hillsides above Hudson Hope.

We swung once more into our saddles. The two horses and Bushman followed the western rim of the tableland, below which occasionally gleamed the creek which, near Steamboat Island in the river behind us, became Dancing Falls. We could just make out the top of this, a moth of mist fluttering in a narrow fold.

"That's the column of ice we saw the last time we walked upriver," I said to Vena.

She nodded. "I guess we can't make out the old mine from here."

"No, it's just at the foot of that far slope, though."

Visible at last, the summit of Bullhead Mountain seemed closer than I had ever seen it. The sight of its nearness made my spine tingle. I tried to picture what it would feel like to stand on its top.

A black bear legged it away from a patch of blueberried juniper bushes ahead of us, but Bushman didn't try to follow, satisfying himself instead with a flurry of barks.

"Smart dog," I said.

"Would it have hurt him?"

"No, he likely could have treed it. But why should he waste the energy? He knows we already have all the bear meat we need."

"How smart do you suppose he really is?" Vena asked after a moment, listening to Bushman's continued barking.

"Well, an Irish wolfhound is one of the most intelli-

gent dogs there is, to begin with. Then, too, you're apt
to get out of a dog what you put into him, and living
alone up here the way we do, we give Bush a lot of our
time. There was a dog at Columbia University one
time, a German shepherd I think it was, that apparently understood about four hundred words of English.
When you stop to think of it, that's a lot. You and I
could do pretty well anywhere in the world if we had
that many key words at our disposal—. What are you
looking at?"

"He's after something."

Then I saw him, too.

"Oh, no!" I said, "and after all that build-up."

Bushman was walking toward us, his face like a
mask.

"What's happened to him, Brad?"

"A porcupine," I said, "and I don't have any pliers
with me. We'd better get on up to the mine where King
can give us a hand. It's lucky none of them got into his
eyes."

"But his poor mouth," Vena said, falling on her
knees beside the dog. "Can't we pull them out with our
fingers?"

"Some of them, sure."

"Perhaps he'll just brush off the rest when he's going
through the bush."

"He can't," I shook my head, getting back on my
horse. "They have barbs on them. If we don't get them
all out, they may kill him. There's the road ahead.
We'd better get to King's."

Whining occasionally, especially when he stopped to
paw at his head, Bushman followed closely.

"He certainly got himself a dose, didn't he?" King
Gething said. He disappeared into a small cabin and
returned with a pair of slim pliers in one hand. "There
should be pretty good light here on the grass in front of
my shack. I didn't know he bothered porkies."

"This is his first one," I said.

"One usually ends it," said King, "but I don't know. From the looks of him, he really lost his temper. That's not a very good sign. I'd better hold him. You can probably do better around his mouth."

With Vena soothing him and King maintaining a grip on his collar, Bushman sat still and let me yank some of the quills from his muzzle. Then the pain began to build up, and he had to be tied as well as held. We didn't keep count, but there must have been at least two hundred quills protruding from his head. Those hardest to get were the ones inside his mouth. I kept that open for Vena by grasping a jaw in each hand and holding it with his lips over his teeth.

"Can't we let those last few go?" Vena asked as Bushman, vainly struggling, let go a shuddering moan. "Won't they work their way out?"

"That's the trouble," King said quietly. "The quills have reverse barbs on them. These keep them working and holding deeper every time the muscles move them. That looks like the last one back there, Brad."

I went over the dog carefully.

"That's it," I said.

Bushman, released, came unsteadily to his feet. He gave a feeble wag of the tail, then ran and plunged his muzzle in the tiny stream that gushed along a narrow chasm beside the mine buildings. Finally, he bounded around the clearing in sheer relief. A minute later he was back drinking again. Then he crowded among the three of us, waiting to be patted.

"How's about a spot of tea?" King Gething asked. "Beforehand, though, I guess we'd better picket the cayuses."

"Any particular place?" I asked.

"That flat just behind my shack here should do fine. There won't be anything for them to get tangled up in, and oats are growing all over the place."

King had been alone at the mine, inasmuch as there would be no big demand for coal again until fall, and he showed us all around. The operation, if small, was spectacular, partly because of the way the log structures perched on the sunny side of Bullhead, whose cliff-banded uppermost slopes lifted enticingly above us.

Everywhere there were evidences of a tremendous amount of hand work, much of it, we learned, the results of largely solitary efforts by King Gething himself. Even the mechanisms for screening the coal had been forged on the spot and were powered by old car engines.

"To run a mine in this wilderness, you don't exactly have to be a combination prospector, miner, surveyor, logger, carpenter, blacksmith, mechanic, inventor, woodsman, freighter, accountant, fireman, and cook," King said, "but it helps."

"How do you ever find time to mine?" Vena asked.

"That's sometimes the problem," King said, and he tightened his belt. "If you'd like to look at the mine, I'll get us some safety lights. I have some batteries charging over in the shack there."

The entry to the mine was across a rough log trestle, below which there were homemade facilities for loading trucks. Wind, swooping down Bullhead, caught up dust that arose under our boots as we went up a small incline. Then we were inside a cold, dark stillness.

The wind behind us took on a hollow sound, and what seemed to be an echo of it was cool against my face. Ties were rough beneath our feet. Vena was beside me, and her hand found mine. Bushman was barking. We called, and he appeared briefly beside us, only to slip away. We heard him barking again outside.

The rusted tracks spiked to the ties were narrow, and they were set closely together as those in the mine below on the river had been.

"That's where I bought most of them," King told us now. "I bought the wheels for the cars there, too."

Now that I thought of it, this tunnel looked a lot like

the one into which we had ventured just above the river level. There was the same ice underfoot and the same thin, clear trickle of water. Although the timbered roof and walls on which our lights shone were new, occasional bulging slabs, and once a splintered prop beside which another had been driven, indicated the deteriorating process already at work.

"Do all mines have drafts?" Vena asked, pushing some hair up under the hard, black hat with which King Gething had furnished her. "There was the same thing in one of the tunnels we went in down by the river."

"They're handy for ventilation where we do have them," King said.

"Didn't I read somewhere that there aren't any dangerous gases in this formation?" I asked.

"That's generally true, but it's always just as well to take as few chances as necessary. Dad was down at the old mine on the river without a light a few years ago. So he lit a match in one of the secondary tunnels. The next thing he knew, there was an explosion all about him. He was pretty well banged up."

"Oh," said Vena. Then she added, "Where does this fresh air come from?"

"You'll see in a few minutes," came King Gething's voice. We passed a glittering black chamber, hollowed out of coal. "Watch your step along here if you don't mind. It's a trifle steep up to the next level."

"Do you find many fossils here?" I asked.

"Quite a few from time to time." King turned as he spoke, and the light on the front of his cap made his face seem long and shadowy. "There's some in the bunk shack if you'd like them. The miners bring them in occasionally."

"What really enthralled Brad," Vena said, and her voice sounded a little too loud, "were those dinosaur tracks. What he really would have liked would have been to bring one back to the cabin."

She laughed, and her laugh seemed a bit forced.

"There's one down there you could get without too much trouble," King Gething was saying, "now that you have horses."

"What's that?" I heard myself saying. "Where?"

"There'd be nothing to it," King went on. "It's intact in itself, as if a blob of mud fell from a dinosaur's foot and hardened just the way it was."

"Does it weigh much?" I asked.

"About forty pounds, I suppose," King told me, pausing. "You could put it in a burlap bag and pack it on a horse without any trouble. I carried it far enough into the main tunnel, the one that had the steel tracks, so the ice wouldn't take it out at breakup. The last time I looked, it was right there on the floor."

"Thank you," I said. "I'd certainly like to pick it up sometime if you don't want it."

"No, you're certainly welcome to it." His light bobbed ahead again. "Here's the shaft."

I realized that the blackness of the tunnel we were now in was relieved by a gray light. Following Vena, I stared upward into a hole at whose top shone the blue sky. Rough rungs led up one side of the opening.

"Is this ladder safe?" Vena was asking.

"Oh, yes," King said. "It comes out on the mountainside, just above the powder shack."

"Then let's go out this way," she said. "I'd like to see everything."

A light wind, turning up the young green leaves of small poplars as it blew down the side of the mountain, seemed to have the smell of spring in it, and I wondered if some part of the departed season still lingered up there on Bullhead's upper reaches. Although these heights seemed close, much closer than we had ever been to them before, they were far enough above us to have snow on them still.

"You think you can see the top from here," King

said, "but you can't. The top rounds off, over above that next canyon to the west, and the cliffs hide it. There'll be snow up there, all right."

"I'd like to climb it sometime," I said. "Is it very hard to climb?"

"Not actually," he said, "not as these mountains go. It's like a lot of things, though. You keep thinking that the next cliff will put you on the top, and then there's another one just beyond. I've always liked to go up right here, between this canyon and the next one. Now, or a little earlier, is the best time of the year, before the bush gets any thicker."

I was studying the slope, figuring that the easiest way to climb beyond the first few bands of rock would be to circle to where they lost their identity near the chasm that was a golden blue depth to the west. When I glanced back, I saw Vena regarding me.

"Why don't we try to make the top tomorrow?" she asked. "It's something we've been wanting to do for a long time."

"All right, that is, if King doesn't mind our staying over another night."

King Gething lifted a hand deprecatingly. "Glad of the company."

"How's about coming along?" I asked.

"I've been," he said. "Besides, you and Vena should go there alone. There's only one first time for something like that."

Bushman was below, nosing about the clearing. The down-currents must have carried either our voices or our scent to him because he began lifting his head inquiringly and barking. Then he started in our direction.

"It's strange he doesn't care for mines," I said. "He always follows us everywhere else."

"I imagine he likes the outside of Bullhead better," Vena said.

"There is a difference," King Gething said, regarding

her soberly. Then he glanced at the sun which was smashing down a pile hammer of radiance through black clouds against a lower slope, scattering dimness that abruptly disintegrated into an upheaval of smoke-trunked poplars. "Both serve to establish an appetite, however."

He extracted a large gold watch from a pocket.

"The enemy has crept up on us," he announced. Below, Bushman had stopped running and was barking at something.

"The enemy?" Vena said.

"The time, as Dudley Shaw calls it," said King. "It's almost seven o'clock. We'd better go down and boil the kettle, or you'll be too famished to climb Bullhead tomorrow."

Bushman was barking wildly, and then suddenly he stopped.

"I guess I'll never get used to these long days," I said, and I began scrambling with them down past the small shack that was the powder house. "It still seems like the middle of the afternoon."

King and Vena were ahead of me.

"Oh, no, Bushman," I heard Vena say.

Then I saw the wolfhound, too.

"Not again!" I exclaimed.

So many porcupine quills covered his muzzle that it looked as if he was grinning at us. He whimpered, though, and slunk close, tail low. Both eyes, fortunately, gleamed clear and unscathed, but the rest of his head actually bristled.

"Well," I said, "I'm glad we've got some help."

He was a pathetic looking sight, and his nerve, understandably enough, did not last long this second session. We had to rope him to an iron cot that King dragged into the clearing. To keep his jaws open while we took turns working on his tongue, mouth, and lips, I got him biting on a stick of kindling, then roped it in place to his collar. Even then I had to pry his teeth further apart, for the back of his mouth was choked with quills.

"How could he possibly get so many?" I asked King.

"He really went in on this one, didn't he?" King said. "Looks as if he just kept on getting angrier. I'd be surprised if he didn't kill it."

"Can an animal do that?"

"Oh, yes," King said. "Fisher, for example, have a trick of turning a porky over so they can get at its bare stomach. Can you tilt his head back just a bit? There we are."

"But he never troubled porcupines before," Vena said, almost crying.

"It happens that way." He straightened for a moment and kneaded his back. "Besides, there's a concentration of porkies around the mine here for some reason."

"That's what I was wondering," she said. "I don't think we ought to stay up here any longer, Brad, not until he's past this stage, anyway."

"All right," I said, "but don't worry. He's going to be all right."

"Maybe he won't be all right the next time. Every time seems to get worse."

"It's pretty late to start back tonight. Then tomorrow there's Bullhead. He's all right. There's nothing to cry about."

"Won't Bullhead wait?" she wanted to know. "We can always come back another time. Besides, I'd be worrying every minute. I couldn't enjoy it."

"All right," I said.

I tried to behave as though it didn't make any difference. Since she felt that way, I told myself, I probably wouldn't have enjoyed the climb, either.

Bushman, head swollen, lay on a heavy fibre mat in one corner of the cook shack that evening. Since there was no longer any need of arising early, we all sat around the big table without regard for the hour and talked. Far below, dimness rose about the land. Once a shower bunched blackly toward us around the shoulder of the mountain, crossed the cabin roof in pattering commotion, then slanted away toward the Peace which was a misty mirror reflecting the sky.

"As Voltaire put it," King was saying, " 'History is the sound of heavy boots going upstairs and the rustle of satin slippers coming down.' "

"Fortunately," Vena said, looking at our comfortably propped feet, "this continent hasn't yet entirely moved beyond the heavy-boots stage of its history."

The river, sky-bright beneath the tiny storm whose tumult must have reached our invisible cabin by now, was a glittering silver street from which rose the occasional hornlike honks of Canada geese.

"It must be getting late," I said.

King reached for a book that I'd noticed lying by his elbow, opened it apparently at random, and slid it toward me.

"Can you read that without a lamp?" he asked.

" 'Much of what we call evil,' " I read aloud, " 'can often be converted into a bracing and tonic good by a simple change of the sufferer's inner attitude from one of fear to one of fight.' "

"Yes, William James," King said. "Now you can tell them back in Boston that you've been living where it's bright enough at midnight to read by daylight."

"Is it really midnight?" Vena asked.

"A few minutes past," King nodded, pushing to his feet. "How about a spot of tea before we begin thinking about turning in?"

In contrast to the winter months, there was now no real darkness to the northern nights, the reason why over a year there were more total hours of daylight here than in regions to the south. Shadows merely lengthened in the stillness until there was a tranquil dusk. This soon brightened again into twilight, as it did that night while I lay awake on the side of Bullhead. It was like after other arduous days when I was somehow so stimulated that, although physically exhausted, I couldn't sleep. Even when I did doze off, in the full light of early morning, I awoke about four a.m.

As on similar occasions, though, I felt fine, and I knew that after a sound sleep the following night, I would be none the worse. Bushman had evidently been waiting for someone to stir. Now he padded across the floor, and I felt his cool nose against my neck. Vena was still breathing regularly. I lay there another moment, looking out the window at Bullhead and wondering if by the time Vena awoke she would have changed her mind about returning that day to the cabin.

I was still thinking about this when I stepped alowly outside, luxuriating in the first oblique warmness of the sunlight. There was a yelp. Bushman was coming back around the cook shack with what I realized was a dead porcupine, evidently the one he had killed the day before. Even as I started to yell at him, he dropped it and backed away from it.

"That settles that," I said. "We do go back today."

There was no sign of King or of any other activity anywhere. I didn't want to arouse Vena to another ordeal and, besides, Bushman seemed to have accumulated only about a dozen quills this time.

Pawing occasionally at his hanging head, he followed me obediently while I got my rope from the saddle. The only way to handle him alone seemed to be to tie him to a tree. When, his nerve now completely gone, he squirmed so violently that I couldn't work on his mouth, I hitched his hind legs as well as his forelegs together and curled him entirely around the trunk. Kneeling on his head, I rapidly completed the task, went over him carefully to make sure I hadn't missed any quills, and then let him go. He took a couple of thankful bounds, then returned and let me stroke a velvety ear.

"Something tells me that you've finally learned your lesson," I told him. "I only hope you'll remember it when we get back up here again."

16

Autumn All Too Soon

"I'd think that by the end of summer particularly, when all the vacationists are going home," one letter said, "you'd wish you were returning to civilization, too."

We didn't see many summer vacationists in the accepted meaning of the word. But a number of geological survey crews, largely staffed with college students, headquartered at Hudson Hope and left from there when autumn approached. Instead of feeling any desire to head toward the cities with them, though, I remembered with a certain amount of pleasure those other occasions, at summer camps and on fishing and hunting trips, when I'd been forced to leave before I'd wanted to go.

Now, at last, I didn't have to join the exodus back to the noise, the gasoline and diesel fumes, and the crowds. No longer was I time-poor. On the way back to the cabin from Hudson Hope on the first day of fall, we tethered the horses and sat beneath a spruce on the sunny river bank for at least an hour, watching a doe and two large fawns racing, dodging, and leaping like playful dogs on an opposite sand spit. Only Bushman was anxious to keep going, but he soon stretched out philosophically where he could keep an eye on everything.

Later, still without any feeling of haste, we stopped to feast on the sweet ripe berries of False Solomon's Seal, while Chinook, who after that one headstrong ride had never given the slightest trouble, nipped the leaves and tips with great relish. Then we found some mature lamb's-quarter.

"That's what I've been looking for," Vena said. "Here, don't let Chinook get it."

"It will be a little tough, won't it?" I said, reining the sorrel away from the patch.

"I want some seeds," Vena said, swinging from her grey to the ground. "I've been writing our friends about how it tastes better than most domestic greens, and one of them has been wondering if it will grow in California."

We salvaged a large envelope from the batch of mail in one of the saddle bags and started filling it with the tiny, gleaming, black discs. After that, we detoured inland to watch a pair of recently arrived beaver working on a dam above the cabin on Bull Creek.

It was while we were comfortably crouched behind willows, warm in the lowering rays of the sun, that I really realized how rich Vena and I had become in time. This was true, furthermore, in an age where— despite increasing conveniences, more and more speed, and shortening work hours—demands on the individual's minutes were restrictively increasing. All at once, I felt wealthy with leisure.

It may have been changing breezes of approaching evening, or one of the beaver may have suddenly seen or heard something. The nerve-tingling smack of a warning tail abruptly cleared the pond of life.

"Come to think of it," Vena said, smilingly accepting my proffered hand and coming to her feet, "I am getting hungry. What are you looking so thoughtful about all of a sudden?"

"I was thinking that back in the city I just used to eat at regular times. I don't think I ever got really hungry."

As we were riding into the clearing with its corral, caches, and the cabin with its woodpiles, I thought again of the millions who'd once more be caged in cities now that summer vacations were over. I was more thankful than ever that Vena and I were here.

Most of the luxuries and many of the so-called comforts of civilization were not only dispensable, I had come to realize, they were positive hindrances. Years were frittered away with detail. Why shouldn't one reduce existence to its essentials and learn what life really had to offer?

From what I'd seen, I knew that for me, at least, a lot more good living was to be bought in the clean, uncluttered reaches of this continent than in any metropolis. In a way, it was as if we were enjoying permanent vacations. Don't many city folk work hard all their lives in the hope of moving some day to the uncrowded spaces?

Sure, quitting the rat race before it quit me meant more work of a kind. I considered this as I began unsaddling the horses and tossing bundles to them, then started carrying in wood and water. All in all, it was work I enjoyed doing.

My outdoor articles, beginning with that one about wild foods and the Chinaman Lake trip, were selling steadily. Our money was going five times farther, and each night we looked forward to getting up the next morning. I'd always had an idea that to maintain oneself on this earth is not a hardship but a pastime if one will live halfway simply. It was working out that way.

Both because of the increasing briskness of the weather and because the wilderness was beginning, with the falling of leaves, to open up again, the pulse of our lives seemed to quicken now with each succeeding day.

A few sportsmen showed up at Hudson Hope, then departed later for their homes after paying in the neighborhood of from sixty to a hundred dollars a day apiece for the enjoyment of the sort of big game hunting that was now mine for no additional expense beyond the few dollars cost of a resident license. A few seemed to regard us with a sort of envy. This couldn't have been because of any financial considerations, certainly, but was, I felt from our own experience, because of the way we could fully enjoy the sort of freedom at which they could only snatch.

"Will you help me with this food list?" Vena asked one nippy morning when our fire was snapping cozily. "I can't make up my mind whether to get dried peaches or dried pears."

"Why not buy a small case of each?" I said.

"It isn't as though we won't have plenty of fruit," she said. "There are dried apples, apricots, raisins, and prunes. And there are the raspberries, strawberries, highbush cranberries, and other things I've put up."

"There's nothing like plenty of fruit with game meat," I said, "and a change is always nice."

"It's just that I don't want to overstock."

She hesitated and seemed about to say something else. Then she bit her lip and looked away.

"Getting everything wholesale the way we are," I said, "there isn't that much money involved. We may as well have the best of everything for as long as we're here. Besides, honey, it isn't as if anything will be wasted. King Gething has told us that he'll be glad to take whatever's left off our hands when we're ready to leave."

"Well," she said, "yes, there's that."

It was fun going over the long list of foods available from the wholesale house in Dawson Creek; sort of like shopping from a big catalog. The illustrations were supplied from our imaginations.

One thing our experience in the farther places had

already taught us was to buy the best of everything. When you figured in transportation, two dollars per hundred pounds to Hudson Hope, plus an additional five dollars to have Ted Boynton bring everything in to the cabin—as well as the work involved in storage and in preparation, reckoned in terms of hours of effort— the initial cost was the lowest price we paid.

Preparing such an order in the wilderness is considerably different from making out a list of groceries in the city. In Boston, for instance, if we miscalculated on evaporated milk, a phone call or at most a quick trip around the corner would remedy the oversight. Here in the woods, on the other hand, it could mean black coffee for the next two months.

The formula we used was based on making a list for an average month, then multiplying it by the number of months for which we wished to outfit. How much cereal, flour, vegetables, fruit, sugar, and so on would we need if we were to dine well for the usual four weeks? What about variety? What about the basics such as salt, spices, etc.?

Then we had to take into account that I might not be lucky enough to get a moose and other big game, although I certainly hoped to do so. The dried bear meat, which had been delicious, was now all gone, so lack of success in future hunting would necessitate laying in enough extra canned meat, fish, dried eggs, and such to make up the main dishes. Such a list, therefore, meant a lot of considering and planning and talking things over.

"How many months shall I order for?" Vena said, tapping her teeth with the pencil and looking out the window.

"Well, let's see," I said, also looking out of the window as if, suddenly, something all engrossing was out there. "We've enough food on hand, haven't we, to carry us into October?"

"Oh, yes, easily."

"Well, then, there's November, December, January, and—. Well, there's part of February." I stopped. "The one year I asked for will end then, won't it?"

She didn't say anything at first. Then she looked up. "I'll sort of miss seeing the geese, and the cranes, and the swans coming back."

"Yes," I said.

"And the ice going out in the spring," she said, "and the poplar buds bursting open like popcorn."

I look at her then. "You really will?"

"After all," she went on, and our eyes met for a moment, "early spring is just about our favorite season."

"Actually," I said, "we were awfully lucky when we arrived here in February that the roads were so good. Some Februarys, Dudley and King have been telling me, people aren't able to get in or out of Hudson Hope for weeks at a time unless they travel by horse or plane."

"Then," Vena said slowly, looking out the window again, "I suppose we'll do just as well to plan far enough ahead so we won't have to depend too much on the weather. Besides, I don't suppose a few weeks one way or the other will make any difference."

"No, I don't suppose they will," I said. I drew a deep breath. "Do you mean you want to leave when the roads will still be smooth and frozen—say, the end of January?"

"Well, not necessarily," she said. "I thought we could wait until the season is well under way—oh, until the latter part of May. If we're going to leave the woods, I don't suppose there's any use in putting up with mosquitoes again." She carefully laid down the pencil. "That is, if you don't mind waiting that long—."

"Me mind?" I said. "Are you sure you won't mind?"

"No," Vena said, "I'll sort of like it. Besides, then we can make our planning and ordering definite. And, well, I really would hate to miss our favorite time of the year."

I was going to say something, but I put my arms around her instead.

Hunting, for those living in the North Woods, is always a matter of compromise. Moose, deer, and such are fattest just before the mating season, which, in the case of moose, the largest deer that has ever lived, is at its height during the frostiness of the full moon in September. The rut of the mule deer follows a month later.

It's when you live back of beyond and are dependent on game meat that you realize how important this fatness is to tenderness, flavor and, most vital of all, to nourishment. Then why doesn't everyone just hunt when the game is plumpest? The difficulty in the wilderness is that if you bring in your game too soon, warm weather may make it difficult to keep and can even dictate canning.

"If possible," I told Vena, "I'd like to wait until just before freeze-up."

"When will that be?"

"It varies different years, so we won't know. I guess I'll just have to wait as long as I can. We want to be eating steaks and roasts this winter. If the cold weather is too long in coming and the game gets too gaunt, we can always buy beef fat from Joe Barkley and add that. Joe says he's going to be butchering."

"Will venison taste all right with beef fat?" Vena wanted to know, somewhat doubtfully.

"It'll taste better than ever. I had some hamburg made one time back in Boston, after a late trip along the Grand Cascapedia River on the Gaspe, by grinding venison with beef fat. It was wonderful. As a matter of fact, if I get a good plump bear, we can use some of that fat the same way."

While I was itching to get out with my rifle, the days

continued warm for week after week. Nights were frosty, perfect weather for beautiful foliage.

Poplars began slowly turning color. Whereas in the spring there had been waves of the lightest green surging over the slopes across river, now it was as if the sea of leaves was suffused with fire from a setting sun. Pools of molten color, salmons and yellows and the deepest of golds, widened in a green ocean composed of lodgepole pine and spruce.

What made the spectacle all the more moving was the fact that the transition was so gradual and so diverse. Near the cabin, one particular poplar at the edge of a small grove rusted, then yellowed, and finally seemed to melt into flame against its still green neighbors. Across the river, the coloration progressed in a similar exciting and always interesting fashion.

The colors nearer the ground were most vivid, the berry bushes with their surplus of sugars running toward scarlets and crimsons, while those richer in tannin deepened more toward purples. The long, slender leaves of the willows yellowed until, in the river breezes, some of them resembled slim clipper ships with sun-gilded sails shimmering.

Hillsides of violet, purple, and magenta fireweed became alive with the wafted gauze of seed-bearing floss.

"It looks almost like frost, doesn't it?" Vena said, one morning when a stronger than usual west wind was curling and wreathing with the white fluff. "Come to think of it, though, there hasn't been any frost for over a week now, and still the leaves continue to change."

"It's because of oxidation rather than frost, you know. It's a matter of pigmentation, like freckling."

Fireweed and other down gathered in the eddies and along the quieter shores of the shrinking river. The water became lower and lower, as a dry spell lengthened and as coldness upriver closed in upon mountain tributaries. Slush, finally, began to heavy the current.

"Noble sight," said Dudley Shaw, standing in the

doorway with us and watching the sun beat gold leaf out of the heavying wavelets. "Freeze-up isn't far away. Better be thinking of *mooswa* before you get bogged down."

It was as if winter was already entrenched in the higher mountains upriver and, summoning strength, was floating down Rocky Mountain Canyon past our cabin.

We awoke mornings now to see long streamers of fog following the current. Dudley Shaw explained that the sourdoughs called them the ghosts of ancient voyageurs, and he said that sometimes he could hear in them old friends talking and laughing. He seemed serious about it, although I don't imagine he really was, and it was true enough that when the wind was right you could make out a sort of rollicking mumble that did sound like paddling fur traders.

This wreathing fog, the forerunner of the mist that would later swirl above open places in the ice, massed higher and higher at dawn between the cooling land and the swollen redness of the sun before finally dissipating into the morning atmosphere.

We were looking at it rise and dissolve one morning, as we strolled over by the corral. Vena watched the still-feeding Cloud and Chinook for a moment, fingers in Bushman's collar. When she turned toward me, the wind from upriver blew a strand of hair across her forehead, and she pushed it back with a graceful gesture.

"What are they going to do this winter when it storms?" she asked.

"What do you mean?" I said. "They'll do what they'd do anywhere else, I suppose—stand with their tails to it."

"But if they were loose," she said, "wouldn't they find a pine grove or some other place where there's protection?"

"I suppose so if one were handy. A lot of times,

though, they'd be ranging where there isn't much of any cover. Horses don't mind storms particularly, Joe tells me. They just eat a bit more to keep warm, that's all."

"Then if we went to the expense of building them a shelter, we'd save money in feed, wouldn't we?"

"All right," I said. "It shouldn't take us more than a few hours to spike something together. We've plenty of slabs left over from the old buildings. I can saw some of the small logs for the frame. Let's see, it'll take four for the foundation, four for the corners, and another four for the top. A flat roof, with what's left of our roofing paper, should do fine."

"Another house," Vena said, and she laughed. "The horses' house."

The building of the shelter was as little trouble as we had anticipated. It took only a short time to hew the tops and bottoms of the base and roof logs roughly flat. Then, with a saw, it required only a vertical and a horizontal cut in each instance to make right-angled notches in their ends.

The foundation logs went into position first. The air bubble in an olive bottle nearly full of water provided a level, the corner of the ax a square. We got everything flat and even. Bracing the four corner posts temporarily into place with slanted slabs, I quickly spiked the frame together.

Heavy slab walls gave the structure rigidity. Once I had nailed additional slabs over each crack, flat side to flat side, the shelter became windproof. With Vena handing up slabs, I put on the roof the same way, with tarred building paper sandwiched between the flat surfaces for waterproofing.

"It still needs something," Vena said, standing back.

"It'll be fine," I assured her. "They can keep dry in there, and it's small enough for their bodies to warm it."

"The doorway," she said. "I've got an idea. That old horse blanket we have. We'll nail it to the top of the doorway so it will fall back into place after they've shoved through."

"That might take some getting used to."

"Don't you see?" she said. "All we'll have to do is feed them in there and they'll have it all figured out. Let's try it now and see."

It worked.

The next morning we got up to a world gemmed in thick frost. Bushman, arising from the warm softness of his home-tanned bearskin rug, shivered.

The skeletal remains of Vena's garden were outlined as if touched along the edges with adhesive and then sprinkled with crushed jewels. Each heavied strand of grass was characterized by its own gleaming fringe. The lingering green of the kinnikinic leaves had become crystalline mats that crackled underfoot. A fresh spider web between the eaves and the east wall of the horses' house sagged with its treasure of frost diamonds.

"What's the temperature?" Vena wanted to know. "I didn't notice."

"It's only a degree or two below freezing," I said. "But you'd better put up a lunch for me anyway."

"You think it's safe to go hunting? The meat will keep?"

"Look at that."

Slush, running heavily now, had so clogged a swirling whirlpool just below a narrow cut in the reefs downstream that water was backing up and skimming with ice.

"But it's rough there," Vena said. "That's the place I thought would freeze last."

"So did I. I thought that the quiet stretches like Box Canyon would harden over first, but Box Canyon is still wide open. I guess it's because all the slush at that point is being concentrated in one small place, and it's acting like a cork in a bottle."

"Pretty soon we'll be traveling the river again," she said, "although this winter, of course, we'll have the horses, too. When is their last load of feed coming in?"

"Ted said he'd pick it up at Matt Boe's during the next day or two. We don't have to worry about the feed. It will be even easier traveling over the trail after it snows." I put an arm around her. "Speaking about food, how's about breakfast?"

"Flippers and tiger?"

"Flapjacks and bacon will be fine. I'd like to get a good early start." We started to walk toward the cabin, the glitter of the river dancing in the trees all about us and the heaviness of the slush like a hush in our ears. "It will be something, won't it, to have the cache filled with all the meat we can feast on until spring?"

"Do you suppose that little herd of moose is still above Box Canyon?" she said, eyes sparkling. "And a bear would be nice, for the lard. I'd like to try making soap with some of the fat, too."

17

Zigzag Wavering To and Fro

There in the snowstorm it was as though I was trying to make my way under deep water. My feet felt as if they were weighted down in cumbersome, lead-heavied boots. Pine trees, amid the froth of wind and flakes, were tall and wavering seaweeds shadowing upward high above me. Over by a knoll, that was like a spin-drift-whitened reef, a wave seemed to break; but it was only a branch curving back into position after releasing its whiteness.

Light came, strangely diluted, into the sifting storm from the open meadow just above Box Canyon, and it seemed as if the cabin must be almost at hand, although everything was just the same; the fresh smell of the snow, the way what remained of the daylight gleamed through it with a sort of incandescence, and the cushioned roughness underfoot.

"Giddap," I said over my shoulder Chinook who jerked at her halter shank, but I had to go back and pass it around a sapling she'd taken on the opposite side.

While I was there I checked the load on her riding saddle and on Cloud's pack saddle. The last of our winter's meat, four oddly-angled moose quarters, was still balanced and secure. I had meant to bring it to the

cache in two trips, but when flakes had started foaming
down, I'd decided to pack my riding horse, too.

"Giddap," I said once more, and when I heard the
creak of the loads and felt the strain on the rope in my
hand ease, I stepped ahead as fast as possible.

Bushman had been standing off to one side, eyeing
us. Now he dipped forward on his front legs and
lunged into a billowing drift. The dive turned to a
wallow and then into a growling, barking roll. The
Irish wolfhound arose, shook himself, nosed the air,
and then dived again. The next thing I knew, he was
up, sniffing a fresh squirrel track, circling a tree, and
barking.

Below to my right, what was left of open river
flowed its black course through a white plain that was
snow-smoking ice. It looked cold.

We circled inland past an old beaver pond. Even
that looked unfamiliar, although the snow falling on
the withered bulrushes had a soft, pleasant sound.
Vena, muffled in a parka, hurried out with short, sliding steps to hold the horses.

I eased their loads to the ground. She volunteered to
unsaddle them and take them out to the corral while I
hung the meat, but I was with her in time to unsheath
my knife and cut the strings of the oat bundles she
tossed to them. Then, arm in arm, with Bushman a
snowy wraith ahead of us, we skidded toward the
cabin.

"I'm glad you're back," she said. "It's snowing
harder, isn't it?"

"Yes, and the flakes are getting smaller," I said. "I
guess we're in for a storm. Why, you weren't getting
worried, were you?"

"Oh, no," she assured me, "it's just that it's so much
cosier here when we're all together. Don't mind about
your feet. I'm going to sweep, anyway."

The cabin had a wonderful apple-like smell to it.

"I found mold on some of the rose hips," Vena said,

"so I decided to put them up. Besides, it was a wonderful day for it."

Warmth enveloped me pleasantly, as I shed my outer clothing and got into fresh, dry woolens. The thought came to me that if I hadn't undergone the discomfort of cold, there would have been no sense of well-being now in getting warm, just as there would have been none in becoming dry again if it weren't for the storm, or in looking forward to the coming supper if I hadn't worked up such an appetite.

"Moose tenderloins?" I asked.

"What about them?"

"I laid a section just outside on the woodpile." I reached an arm out into the cold. "Here they are. I thought you might like them for dinner tonight."

"It's just the weather for them."

The swarm of flakes tumbling against the windows brought an increased awareness of isolation. Flour and cereal sacks, I realized comfortably, bulged plumply in the cache by our log cabin. Game quarters, marbled with fat, promised many a sizzling steak and savory roast. The bear fat Vena had wanted was there too.

Under the trapdoor at my feet, safely below frost level, were potatoes, turnips, carrots, cabbages, and other delicious perishables that had grown tender and delectable in Vena's garden during the long hours of daylight. There were bunches of wild onions, and the other free foods, too, and the jars of wild preserves and jams. Just the thought of them made my mouth start to water.

Then there was the wood cut and stacked outside, the fuel for the lamps, and the other necessities we had stored and ready.

"You know one thing we're getting back here," I said to Vena, "that we nearly lost in the city?"

She had been scalding some jars, but now she stopped and smiled at me. "Which one do you mean?" she asked.

"Freedom," I said.

"You tried to tell me that back in Boston, didn't you?" she said. "I couldn't understand it. Even if I had, I guess I wouldn't have believed it."

"I'm not sure I entirely believed it myself," I said, "not really. There's been another thing about this life, Vena. Even though we may go back, we'll never be quite the same again.

She stood still.

"After this, certainly, I'd never want to get back into the grind of show business."

"You can be a housewife now."

"I've been thinking of that," she said. "But with all the time-savers, what would I ever do with all the time I'd save?"

"I don't know," I said. "I don't even know if I can stand working for a tradepaper again, either."

"You won't have to, not with the way your stories and articles are selling now."

"Yes, there's that. The only trouble, Vena, is that the ones that have gone over have all been about this life here."

"You're not going to forget about the wilderness just because we happen to be back in Boston," she said.

"No, but there may be more to it than that. It's one thing to be making your way home through the woods at night with the help of the North Star, with Orion, Cassiopeia, and the Big Dipper all wheeling around it. It's another to glance up at all that from the Esplanade, with the air filled with fumes, and lights all about, and any number of streets surely pointing the way back."

I heard her catch her breath sharply.

"Do you think we can be happy there again?" she asked.

"I don't know," I said. Then I said, "Yes, I do, too. Of course, we can be happy."

"I'm not so sure, darling," she said. "Are you sure?"

I put my arm around her. I could feel the muscles in her back moving, as if she was trying to keep them still but couldn't. I could hear the rush of the storm against the windows. "You and I can be happy anywhere," I said.

"But it won't be the same, will it? A wild animal is probably happy after being born in a zoo. But I wonder what it would be like to give it a taste of wilderness, then bring it back again?"

"We can reason better than a wild animal. It's something to have faced the fundamentals for once, even if we don't have to any more, and to have proven we're capable of meeting them."

"Maybe that's what I'm afraid of," she said. "Maybe I'm the sort of person who has to go on proving herself."

There was a full moon that night that glowed through the clouds and the scurrying snow, and I remembered how before we'd come North I used to dread what I'd thought of as the dismal, long, dark winter nights. This night was soft with a radiant whiteness that, I knew, would continue for as long as the lengthiest sun-brightened day of June.

"Remember John Greenleaf Whittier?" Vena said. "'A night made hoary with the swarm/and whirlwind dance of the blinding storm,/as zigzag wavering to and fro/crossed and recrossed the winged snow.'"

It was that, exactly, I thought, looking out at where lamp light extended a luminous path along which the airy flakes danced. There was a sense of privacy to it all. More than ever, we had become a small secluded world.

It was, I suppose, an outcrop of the realization that from the time he can reason, each of us has obligations to others and to society as a whole. When you are totally isolated physically, however, for the moment remote from all but the most basic distractions and restricted by no laws but those imposed by night and

snow and cold, it's as though any such duties cease
and, for awhile, you can live an entirely individual
existence.

Snow still rasped against the stovepipe the next
morning. The whitened horses loomed up like whinnying ghosts when I hurried out to the corral to toss them
their bundles. Bushman made his rounds quickly. He
was ready to come in again when, my chin cold against
the snow-sheathed firewood that filled one arm, I
shoved the door open ahead of me.

"The rabbits will eat well today," I told Vena, dump-
ing the load of wood into the box.

"I thought they'd pretty well cleaned up what they
can reach," she said, setting the oatmeal back on the
stove.

"That's the point. The snow will act like a stepladder
and let them reach higher and higher."

Snow was falling almost vertically now about the
cabin, balling its white fists on the evergreens and extending its blanched arms and fingers along the slim
black bones of poplar limbs. Along the river below,
however, wind was blowing, marking the gracefulness
of its curves in creaming snow.

Our conversation kept running through my mind, as
I wound a fresh sheet of paper into the typewriter.
Then it began to fall into rhythm with the click of the
keys and the thud of the space bar.

Why, after all, should it be necessary to set up
housekeeping in the midst of the northern winter just
to remain secluded? It wasn't as if, alone and strange,
you couldn't be just as lonely walking on crowded
Tremont Street as along the wildest river. Then I decided the point was that no one could expect to be
comparatively free who tarried in the proximity of
everyday habits and pressures.

"I'll just be out around," Vena was saying. "I want
to get outdoors, and I may as well brush out the paths
before the snow gets too heavy."

"All right," I answered. I hadn't noticed that she'd been putting on her brown ski pants, boots, and red eiderdown jacket. Even now, I couldn't quite believe she looked so well in them. "As soon as I get finished here, I'll be out."

One thing that is absolutely essential to successful living together in the wilderness, I thought now, is respect of inner privacy. This is necessary for happiness anywhere, of course, but particularly in a small cabin where, if either of us infringed on the integrity of the other, living could quickly become intolerable.

We were fortunate, I supposed, that we had both found a common ground on which, although thrown intimately together, we could meet without wrenching the other out of shape. We each had our own private nooks, such as the shelves on which I kept my papers, where the other never trespassed. When one of us was going about personal chores, too, we'd got so that the other paid it no more attention than if it were happening on another floor and in another room.

Vena had secured the stiff broom we'd made by lashing birch wands to an old handle, and I saw she was making the snow fly. Bushman, barking, was leaping after the white smother. Watching the rhythm of her motions, I realized again how much beauty there was in the commonest of things, and I turned once more to my typewriter. I wanted to complete my writing schedule for the day and be out there, too.

The storm came to an end that afternoon, delineated by the low-angled sun in such a way that the wind seemed filled with starlight. Then, with the approach of evening, the wind stopped, too, and stillness descended from Bullhead again like an invisible cloud. High above, an eagle wheeled slowly. Up in what remained of the sunlight, its gilded planing seemed to stress the silence of the snowy realms.

"Isn't it peaceful?" Vena asked.

"Except for the dawns, this is still the part of the day I like to be outdoors best."

Then small birds brushed through the dusk and landed on and about Bushman's obscured food pan. The wolfhound set up a barking that, from close in among the foothills, was answered by a sharp, tremulous, whining quaver.

"I wonder what the coyotes are singing at?" Vena said.

"Maybe they're just being neighborly," I answered. "There are worse neighbors."

The plaint died away. The birds, scattered by Bushman, vanished. Scuffing through the squeaking snow with Vena toward where the stack of oat bundles was an igloolike whiteness, I felt the quiet and the solitude of the northern mountains in wintertime. Bushman was ahead somewhere, and for the moment even the horses were standing still. There was a kind of comfortable security about it all, a certain profound peace whose harmonious majesty seemed somehow to emanate strength. It was all good, I thought, and it was ours.

"It'll be Christmas soon," I said. "Is that what you were thinking about, our first Christmas in the woods?"

"Actually, I was wondering what the birds eat after snow has covered the ground."

"Oh, highbush cranberries, rose hips, seeds, and such."

"It must be hard for them."

"I guess so," I said. "But, then, they're used to having it hard. Easy living never made anyone or anything successful or happy. A lot of times, it's the other way around."

"I know, but it's nice to help out, too, when we can. And it would be fun."

I suppose our idea for an outdoor Christmas tree was born then. A sturdy one was growing fragrantly between the cabin and the river, in full view of the windows. Since growing old enough to go away to school, I'd never put in much time on preparations for the holidays. Now I was surprised when helping Vena ready the decorations really did turn out to be fun.

These ornaments consisted of such edibles as red strings of cranberries, little foil cones that we filled with tidbits such as crumbs and bits of suet, and even a topping star that I hacked from bacon rind. We put them all high, beyond Bushman's reach, and later Vena baked some hard Christmas cookies in all sorts of interlocking shapes, iced them colorfully, and suspended them from wires.

The birds found the holiday feast first. In the red of the first dusk it was there we saw the snowbirds sitting as if draped in a long strand over the tree, shimmering like a necklace of pearls.

Later, a small thin weasel, all white except for a black tip to his tail, made a series of passages through the snow to the base of the tree where fragments of food were always falling. We came to call him Herman the Ermine, and it was always amusing to see him slip into one hole and then, almost instantly appear from another. Field mice tracks, intricate as filagree, were frequent, and we thought we could recognize a quartet of visitors who always appeared about four o'clock in the afternoon and whom we knew as Petey, Henry, Patricia, and Henrietta.

Probably the most consistently amusing visitor, though, was a red squirrel that somehow got named Sammy. Even Bushman became accustomed to Sammy, who used to scamper from tree to tree and from woodpile to woodpile in making his studied approach, and who adopted as his special project the task of cutting each cookie loose and hauling and dragging it to his caches somewhere inland. Sammy would sometimes become so intent on the difficult job of gnawing free a particular creation that, often clinging upside down to the swaying confection itself, he'd occasionally tumble and bounce with it to the snow.

The last cookie was finally detached and transported away, and Sammy transferred his attention to the glittering foil cones that Vena kept filled with small odds and ends from our meals, mixed with a nourishing base of dry rolled oats. Coincidentally, as he got better acquainted with these new surroundings, Sammy became more of a character. He eventually acquired the habit of scratching at our windows early winter mornings while we were still abed, stopping only after Vena had got up to refill the foil containers perhaps emptied by a wind during the night.

That early storm was the only one of the winter that amounted to anything. All season we rode regularly to town for the mail and to wherever else we fancied. The horses were irrevocably ours by now. I'd bought Cloud sometime before, but Gene Boring had been reluctant to conclude a deal for Chinook. Later, I found Vena had encountered the same difficulty when she'd tried to purchase Cloud. What we'd secretly done, of course, had been to buy the other's favorite mount for a Christmas present to the other.

Spring came closer. As the time for our return to the city neared, our activities became more and more feverish. It was as if both of us wanted to live deep, and suck out all the marrow of life, while we were still where we could.

18

Breakup

If it had not been for the increased tempo of our lives, we probably wouldn't have gone for that dinosaur's footprint King Gething had told us about.

"You know you'd like to get it," Vena said. "There's no reason why we shouldn't, but we've got to hurry. With all this warm weather, the breakup can't be far away. Then the river will rise, and we won't be able to get there until too late."

"I suppose that we could put it in a sack," I said, "and tie it to my saddle."

"The way there's no snow this year," Vena said, "we can ride from King's almost to the old mine. It'll be a wonderful souvenir. Besides, if we don't get it now, we may never have another chance."

"Probably not," I admitted.

"Brad," Vena said, "will you do something for me?"

"What?" I asked.

"Our time here is almost up. Let me do the things with you that you want to do most."

"All right, if that's what you really want."

"That's what I'd like to do most," she said, "in the time we have left."

I wasn't sure what day it was when we left for King Gething's because, except for the mail, time, as such, didn't mean much here in the wilderness, and we couldn't decide whether it was a Monday or Tuesday. Anyway, no one was at King's mine, although everything was open. It was still morning, because we'd got an early start, so we left our bedrolls in the building where we'd stayed before and continued on down an old trail to the river.

It was as lovely a spring day as we'd ever experienced in the North, warm and golden blue. The sun was glinting on the icy skin of the river. This looked bunched and swollen, as if corded currents just beneath were straining for action. Swallows were already in the narrowness of Box Canyon just downstream, wafting like petals across the wind.

Daylight, hard and bright and clear, followed us a short way into the tunnel, like light slanting off a white farmhouse. Then, as obscurity deepened, it was as if evening was approaching us from the other extreme of the subterranean passage.

I don't know how long we hunted for the rock containing the imprint of the dinosaur's foot because there was a sort of fascination to it all. This was compounded partly by the collision of modern and ancient history; of the relatively new coal mine, closed down less than a dozen years before, and of the great reptiles who had wallowed here during cretaceous eons when this had been a steaming swamp.

King Gething had indicated that the fossil would be easy to find. What he hadn't taken into account, I guess, was the way other rocks had become dislodged from roof and walls and how ice had built up during years of seepage. We were still looking, and paying little attention to Bushman's barking and other outside noises, when there was a growing rumble.

It was a queer sound, both grinding and thunderous, which so enveloped us here in the tunnel that it seemed to be bursting from the interior of the earth. Vena was gripping my arm, and the noise was persisting and

swelling until the ground itself appeared to be rever-
berating. The tremendous roar came closer, with rum-
blings and crunchings that shook my very bones. Then
these suddenly seemed muffled.

"What is it?"

"I don't know," I said, and I was shoving her ahead
of me. "It sounds like an earthquake. Let's get out of
here."

The light seemed more diffused and dimmer than I
remembered, and I supposed that we must have been
further under Bullhead Mountain than I had thought.
Then I felt water about my feet. Ahead was ice. I
remembered the cakes of the year before, some as large
as small cottages. Those moved in front of the tunnel
now by the rising river seemed as formidable, even
though I hacked ineffectually at them with my short
prospector's pick I'd brought this time.

"Can't you get through?" Vena was saying. "Here,
let me try with this pole."

But it was no use.

"You're not giving up, are you?" she asked.

"It isn't that." I tried to sound encouraging. "It's just
that there is probably an easier way out. For one thing,
there must be a ventilation shaft like the one in King's
mine. Let's find it."

I found out something about myself during the next
few moments. The walls of the narrow passage seemed
to be pressing in against me. The feeling had been
growing steadily, I realized. It had even had a sort of
fascination, particularly because I'd been able to wall it
off as long as there had been daylight to assure me.
Now that blackness closed in, it was as though I were
being smothered.

Vena was so close behind that she bumped into me.
For a desperate instant, I tried to shove the rock away
from her with one hand. I wrenched the flashlight from
my pocket.

Its beam scattered startlingly, setting up an array of

shadows. I became convinced we had stopped on the edge of a void, and I held Vena back with one arm, all the time trying to appear calm. When I sorted out the shadows, though, I saw we were still in a comparatively level area, although there was rubble at our feet where a slab in the roof was tilting downward.

"Watch your step," I said, quickly turning the light back on the floor. It didn't sound like my voice. "Keep close to me."

"Don't worry," she said, and it didn't sound like her, either.

The pitch was so gradual as to be almost level. Water splashed about our feet. But that, too, I thought, was a boon because of the way it made our rubber-soled boots cling more surely to the accumulation of ice from the continual overflow.

Then I began wondering if, even for springtime, there wasn't an awful lot of overflow. I came to a sudden halt and held the beam downward. A dirty trickle of slush-flecked river water was surging among our feet.

Whether or not it was because the sight caused the muscles in my hands to contract, or if it was because my palms became even more moist, I don't know. But, suddenly, the smooth metal cylinder of the flashlight seemed to be slipping from my fingers. The thought of enveloping darkness so unnerved me that I clutched the light with both hands.

"What's the matter, Brad?"

I thought of the wire ring at the back of the case.

"I just want to fix something," I said.

After a moment of fumbling, I unsnapped the ring. I found a hank of rawhide in a pocket. It was long enough so I could suspend the flashlight from my neck, yet continue to direct it with a hand.

"There," I said, and I tried to give a matter-of-fact laugh, although the water had risen about our boots even during those few moments. "Let's find that shaft."

"All right." Then she said, "Don't worry about me."

I put an arm briefly about her, then let her go again and continued gingerly ahead. It was getting colder the farther we ventured under the mountain. Even that short wait had numbed my fingers. I became more and more aware of this insidious new enemy when I reached cave-ins whose scaling required the use of both hands.

Once a projection of sandstone crumbled in my fingers. Holding grimly with my other hand, I was swung hard against the wall. There was a tinkle, as glass in the flashlight shattered. The darkness became absolute.

"What's the matter?" Vena called, her voice lifting hollowly.

"Nothing," I said. "Stay where you are."

"I heard glass."

"It's the flashlight. I've another bulb, though. Stay where you are."

I wedged myself where I could have both hands free and tried to relax. It was difficult in the dark to unscrew the remains of the broken bulb. It was even more unnerving to replace it with the spare from the back of the case.

The realization kept plaguing me that I had brought only this one extra bulb. Suppose it should fall while I was trying to extract it from its cotton batten? Then I finally had it started in place, and I began thinking, suppose it wouldn't light? I pressed the switch. Nothing happened. I shoved the switch harder, then in the opposite direction. Suddenly, brilliance was all about us again.

Then, I thought, suppose I should break this bulb? There was no longer any lens over the face of the flashlight for protection. It would be dangerous to leave it dangling loosely around my neck now when I had to resort to both hands to get us over the fallen rocks that were becoming increasingly prevalent.

"We're going to try something else," I told Vena, and I added, "It'll save the batteries."

"Aren't the batteries all right?" The coldness seemed to be constricting the normal range of her voice, and the words sounded queerly small and tight. "I thought I saw you putting in new ones back at the cabin."

"They weren't new," I said, trying to get some heartiness into it, "but they're fine. We just want to keep them that way. Here's what let's try if you don't mind."

Another pile of rubble was looming close; a jumble of coal, slabs of clay ironstone that were yellowish in the artificial gleam, and moisture-darkened pebbles, all slanting from a precariously sagging section of roof. I stood still and carefully searched out my next few steps where, tight against the one still intact wall, I could brush past the splintered timbers with the least possible contact.

"Now, don't move," I told Vena. "Wait while I go ahead. You'll be all right."

"You're not going to leave me?"

"Of course not. It'll be just a moment."

With the route fixed in my mind, I forced myself to snap off the flashlight. It felt cold against my chest when I shoved it within my shirt. Then I proceeded as far as I could in the darkness until cautiously extended arms indicated that the tunnel was clear again. I flashed the electricity back on, and Vena groped almost frantically after me.

"I don't much like this," she said when she was at my side.

"We shouldn't have to go much further. Feel that draft? It's getting stronger all the time."

We kept proceeding wherever necessary by the same short stages. The going was increasingly rough. Still, it remained gradual enough not to become impossible. On the other hand, I realized the very moderateness of the ascent was letting flood water build up higher about our feet.

Then the feeling of being closed in began getting worse every time the darkness shut down around me once more. The pressure on my body seemed to become so heavy that I could scarcely find enough air to breathe, although all the time I was struggling to maintain a matter-of-course exterior. When the tunnel became even more constricted, strangely enough I was not entirely sorry. At least, it would mean that I would have to keep the light on all the time. I shortened the thong to prevent it from swinging too far from my body in case I should suddenly lose hold on it.

I became more and more aware of the roaring river behind me, the scrape and squeak of rubber-soled boots beneath me, and the quick, loud, weighty heartbeats within me. A film of ice reflected the yellow beam in such a way that a long black immensity seemed to leap from one of the many side passages. Perspiration sprang out coldly all over me. Then I saw it was my own shadow.

"Are you all right?" Vena said.

"Yes," I said, and then I wished I could have just nodded instead, for I couldn't keep my voice steady. "I'm just a little cold."

"Do you suppose Bushman got away all right?"

"Oh, yes." The handle of my prospector's pick rattled against the wall when I turned to look at her, and I shoved the wooden handle more securely into my belt. "He'd only have to run a few yards down the shore to get up on the bank."

"I haven't heard him barking."

"Well," I said, "we are in quite a way."

Coal glittered blackly on both sides of the tunnel. Occasional entries along its upriver length were darker blobs of shadows, but the decaying ties at our feet kept us straight. I shrank back at what looked like a skeleton shining whitely ahead. When I forced myself on, I saw it was a mass of bleached poles and sticks that had apparently floated in here at one time, then became wedged at this particular point.

"Do you suppose we have to go much further?" Vena said, drawing beside me.

"Not this way," I said slowly, playing the light through the wood.

"What do you mean?"

I shone the beam wordlessly. A solid vertical wall showed why the drift had concentrated at this spot. The ties, too, came to an end.

"There isn't any way out, after all."

"There's got to be a way out," I said.

"Yes, the way we came in. We may as well go back."

"No, wait, Vena."

"What's the use? Perhaps we can take some of these poles and smash the ice away from the entrance."

"There's the water, too," I said, trying to straighten out my thoughts. "The river is backed up below here, probably in Box Canyon. It did that last spring, remember?"

"We've got to do something," she said in too tight tones. "No one has any idea we're here. They're not apt to know for days or weeks."

"We're going to do something, honey." When I put an arm around her, I could feel she was tense and trembling, and this somehow steadied me, for someone had to be steady. "There's got to be another way out. King told us about ventilation shafts. The draft must be coming from one."

"We don't know that," she said. "Besides, I don't even feel a draft any more."

It took me a moment to realize she was right.

"That's it," I said.

"What?"

"Don't you see?" I said. "The shaft must run out of one of those last few side tunnels we passed."

"But how can we tell? Anyway, the flashlight seems

to be getting weaker. Pretty soon we won't even have a light."

I shoved the switch, and blackness reached for us.

"We could do it even without a flashlight," I heard myself saying. "All we have to do is find the draft again, then follow it. Are you ready to get started?"

"I'm ready," Vena shivered, and she drew her hands resolutely back as the light snapped on again.

The splashing of water beneath our feet, and the way it sloshed and rippled around our ankles, took on a weird, misshapen hollowness. The sound echoed eerily about us, as we turned back the way we'd so laboriously come.

Perhaps it was because of the fact that we were now advancing against the main flow, but the coldness seemed to be pulling more strongly at my numbed legs. The electric beam, striking the slush-heavied surface, danced crazily ahead of us.

The vacancy that was the side excavation down which fresh air was pouring appeared sooner on the upriver side of the main tunnel than I had dared hope. I could see now why we had given it only brief attention our first time past. Unpeeled props on one side of the heavy plank roof had given way, allowing the overburden to angle downward so acutely that only a narrow egress remained.

"I'd better go alone," I said.

"If you go, I want to go, too."

"It isn't that," I said, "but there may not be room to get through. Then if there isn't room to turn around, either, we might have a hard time both getting out."

"Oh," she whispered.

"Don't worry," I said. "I won't get very far away from you."

Crawling on my stomach, I hadn't squirmed more than a few feet before the flashlight became such a nuisance that I had to slip the thong from around my neck. It was easier to extend the light ahead of me while I inched forward, hunching ahead whenever I could on knees and elbows.

The batteries were becoming so dim now that I reverted to the former practice of briefly scouting out the passage in front, then proceeding in darkness. I was crawling ahead with increasing speed when the dragging loop must have caught on a projection. The next think I knew, the smooth metal cylinder was jerked out of my hand. I heard it thud, then clatter.

"Are you all right?" Vena's voice came.

"Sure," I made myself say, "sure."

"I can't see your light any more."

Echoes contorted the words.

"Stay where you are. It'll be all right."

Pushing cautiously to my knees, I kept groping frantically about me. Then I forced myself to stop and go at it methodically, working over the tunnel around me inch by inch, first in front and then to either side. There was nothing. I felt for a large rock, anything, with which I could mark my present position so as to be able to come back to it if casting further ahead was not successful.

It was while searching behind me, after being unsuccessful in other directions, that I encountered the leather lace. My fingers followed it cautiously to the welcome cold smoothness of the metal.

Relief made my whole body go loose when the flashlight was again in my hands. I pressed the switch. I pulled and shoved at it harder. Then, reluctantly, I felt for the bulb. Only a tiny ring of jagged nothingness awaited my investigating finger.

19

Bullhead Mountain

The darkness, pressing downward under the weight of Bullhead Mountain, seemed to have a thousand stifling hands. I felt stranger than I ever have before in my life. All at once, I had to get to where I could see something. A wall hit me. I got straightened around again in the direction of the draft. Then I clawed and wriggled ahead through the dark tunnel that because of cave-ins suddenly seemed to be shoving me almost flat, nearly pinioning my arms.

My head came up against the roof before I had proceeded very far. The contact knocked me prone. Even as I was shaking off dizziness, I realized I was still hunching forward.

I ducked to avoid a sharp projection. In my excitement, the understanding of what that meant escaped me. It was moments before I realized I could now distinguish between the greater and lesser blackness of rock and air.

By that time, I was over still another mass. I was threshing forward on my stomach because that was the only way I could keep going here. The increased dampness of the narrowing rock all about soaked through my clothing. Its chill increased the numbness in my hands. That had a good side to it, too, I decided with almost a laugh, for it deadened the rawness of them.

Water dropped on me now with a cold, somehow ominous drip. The splash of the drops on the stone took on a harsh, smacking intensity. Then I realized I could stand. Far above, light made odd, dim patterns. I had the sudden, hope-draining fear that I had reached the shaft only to discover it useless because its top had somehow been sealed. Then I understood that what must have happened was that it had become choked with vegetation at ground level.

"It's here," I called to Vena, "I'm coming back to get you."

I found that what I wanted to do least in the world was to venture back into that forbidding concavity. It gaped in the side of the shaft like a sinister wound. Then I heard Vena's answering voice, and I was hastening toward it. Matches, when I could shield them sufficiently, helped some, especially when she was with me and we were on our way back, although their assistance in the jagged obscurity was mainly to our morale. The primary assistance was rendered by the onrushing cold air, although it was this that made each new plume of flame an insecure, fluttering barrier between us and the conspiring darkness.

Once the deceptive gleam, which I was endeavoring to keep the draft from separating from the matchwood, caused me in its last waverings to choose the wrong slit in the tunnel ahead.

I couldn't have thrust myself forward more than a few yards before rock, ahead of me everywhere I could move my hands, brought me to a sickening standstill in the darkness. Momentary terror poured over me, so hotly that I became wildly aware that there was no longer any cooling draft; that only inert air, trapped beneath the suspended burden of Bullhead Mountain, now surrounded me.

I started to wriggle backwards, but then I felt Vena's

hands against my ankles. A choked, imponderable resonance was all about me. I listened to it dully before I realized it was my own voice, oddly calm, telling her she must go back.

"But I can't," she was saying. "I can't turn."

Then she wanted me to strike a match. I tried vainly to work one hand down to my match case, even after I realized that this dead end might be triggered with explosive gas. Reason asserted itself, finally, and I just lay there, trying to retain enough self-control to make her understand that this was a bottleneck.

When I eventually felt the pressure against my legs easing, I made myself stay still so I wouldn't inadvertently kick her while propelling myself backward. There didn't prove to be enough space in which to do anything, however, except to try to get enough purchase with my toes to draw myself backwards. I didn't seem to be accomplishing any more than to force myself from side to side, the way you try to loosen a cork in a bottle. Then she was tugging at my feet. I scarcely realized that my face was scraping against the rock. One of my knees found a purchase. Then I was where I could move, and stretch, and breathe.

Nothing in the tunnel seemed really bad after that except the fear that I might somehow lead us into another *cul de sac*. The fresh air kept me straight, though. It was only moments before we stepped into the shaft.

There had been a ladder once, but this had rotted over the years and now lay in a damp clutter where we stood. I tested a rung with a foot. It broke soddenly.

"How far up is it?" Vena asked.

"It's hard to judge in this light. I don't think it's as far as it looks; probably sixty feet or so."

"At least, the water can't get us here," she said. "Can't we just wait until the jam is broken?"

"How will we know when that happens without going back? And I don't want to be caught in there

again. Besides, we're in no shape to wait." I moved the
prospector's pick around to the front of my belt. "I can
make it."

"It's too dangerous."

"We can't both just stay here," I said, "and I've
probably the better chance."

I tried to rub some feeling back into my hands
which were becoming more numb. The cold, too, was
reaching the muscles of my body. Our move, whatever
it was, had to be soon. Shifting my short pick to where
I could grasp it more easily, I started to climb.

The rock was damp enough to be slippery. In spite
of that, I did well enough at first. At two critical stages
I even managed to jam my toes into little funnel-like
cavities, probably worn by water as they were similar
to those that had pocked our waterfall each winter.

But although I could use the pick to make the holds
surer, gripping with just one hand while I worked became more and more awkward. For one thing, it usually left me too close to where I was picking to proceed
efficiently. There was the danger, too, of getting a rock
fragment in an eye.

My hands ached. My muscles seemed to have become hot wires. Then, worse, my fingers began to lose
their sense of feel. I missed a hold and saved myself
only by dropping the tool.

"Watch out!"

It seemed to fall a long way before thudding on the
bottom.

"Are you all right?" I called.

"I'm fine."

It looked a long way back, but I could gauge by
glancing upward that I was no more than a third of the
way out. While I was still able, I made my way down. I
collapsed there on my back and tried to regain my
strength. Then Vena was sitting beside me and holding
my head in her lap.

"No go?" she asked quietly.

"It's not far. I can make it."

If the sides of the shaft were only closer together, I thought, staring up into the dimness. Then I could climb them almost as if they were ladders, resting when I needed by bracing myself in the space between. I had a momentary vision of the iron fire escapes of Boston's Gloucester Street. If only I had one of those old black ladders here!

Then I sat upright. "Why don't I make my own ladder?"

"That lumber is all rotten. There's nothing here nearly long enough, either."

"I don't mean that kind of a ladder. I'll be right back."

Excitement overrode my fatigue. It seemed to take only minutes to drag three sound poles from the driftwood wedged along the way we had come. I trimmed the seasoned spruce to the desired lengths with my knife. I wedged the first pole between the narrow walls of the shaft, not far from the bottom. The second pole I worked into position about twenty inches above it.

I put my weight gingerly on the first pole. Then I eased myself upright, steadying myself by leaning my knees against the second pole. With the help of the pick, I was able to seat the third pole snugly about the same distance above the second.

Holding to the wall and to the third pole, I stepped up onto the second. I reached back down for the first. Then what had been the first rung of my improvised ladder became the fourth rung, and so on.

"It'll go," I said. "Watch out for your eyes. You'd better get back in the passage in case any rock falls."

"Oh, be careful."

I worked higher and higher with the three poles. These sometimes assumed exaggerated tilts, for it was not always practical to set them level. The main thing was to get them solidly into place.

I had to stop frequently to ease my muscles. I found that I could rest with reasonable comfort. This I did by straddling the middle pole, with my feet on the one below and with my hands clasped around the one above.

The visions that welled up in me when I dangled there in the greyness cramped my stomach. No matter how grimly I clung, the depth became a macabre black magnet tugging me downward. Even when the overgrown mouth of the shaft came closer, the light that worked in through the heavy vegetation did little more than make the emptiness a duller, dirtier grey than the rock itself.

"Are you all right?" Vena called once when it had taken longer than usual for my strength to come back.

"Everything's fine."

I was going to say it again, because it didn't seem as though the queerly misshapen words could have reached her. Then I saw a shadow move in the bottom of the shaft, and I heard, "You're more than halfway."

"It's hard to judge up here." The dullness of my reaction told me more than I wanted to admit of my state. "You'd better stay back in the tunnel. Stuff is falling all the time."

"I'm staying back except when you stop. Don't think about me."

My weariness continued to increase the higher I laddered upward. That, however, wasn't what troubled me most.

The hardest part of the operation was to secure the lowest pole after I'd climbed above it. The steadiest way to do this proved to be straddle the middle pole and to grasp the uppermost pole with one hand. I discovered that I could help some with my feet in working the lowest one free with my other hand.

As I got higher, though, the way the faint light reached endlessly below struck me with uncertainty. I fought against the feeling. Then I began to shake. All I could do then was to clench the top pole with both hands and just sit there. I had the conviction that if I moved even a fraction of an inch, my balance would go and I wouldn't be able to do anything to stop falling.

I clung there in space, eyes clamped tight to shut out the dark. The weakness finally left me. Shaking, I continued upward. Then another dizzy spell immobilized me. It took longer to recover from this one.

The ascent became an unbelievable horror. I tried to retrieve the bottom pole without looking down. After it had almost slipped from my grasp, I gave that up.

The play of shadows farther and farther below kept dragging at my attention, warning me of the increasing penalty of a false move. Despite the cold which left me numb and stiff, my fingers were now continuously moist. I kept drying them against my clothing, fearful lest a pole might slip through them.

It happened with a rapidity that held me paralyzed. I'd had to tug with all my strength to get one end of the lowest rung to leave its niche. The length of spruce gave all of a sudden. The other end swung so hard against the wall that the wood bounced from my grip.

I froze at the thumping, scraping descent, my warning yell to Vena echoing about me. The fall was followed by a clump that might have been the wood striking her.

"Vena!"

"What happened?"

"Did that hit you?"

"No, no. What was it?"

"Just one of the poles," I said.

My glance wavered upward. There were about fifteen more feet, I surmised. The worst part of it was that the last half of this seemed absolutely bare and smooth. I told myself, without much conviction, that this might be only a trick of light.

The loss of that one pole made the ascent harder out of all proportion. What I had to do now was sit, place my back against the wall, and get as much of a hand-grip as I could in some irregularity. It wasn't too bad loosening the pole beneath the one on which I was seated. But then I had no second rung to support me while I fixed the upper pole in place.

My nerves stretched tighter. The pole on which I depended seemed to be arching beneath my weight, or rattling insecurely in its sockets, or splintering loose. Still, I made my way upward.

Once when I was waiting out a dizzy spell, I thought I heard Bushman barking in the distance. But when I listened, there wasn't anything but the subdued roar of the river, the whine of wind above, and my pounding heart. Wearily slipping the short pick again out of my belt, I deepened a hole above me. Then, feet on the lower pole and hands on the upper, I sidled across the abyss to perform the same task on the opposite wall. Finally, I went through the routine of moving up one more rung.

There I stopped. The rock formation had changed. A hard, even surface extended from where I was cling-ing all the way to the top. The blunted steel point scarcely made a mark on it. I stared upward at the rim. Even if I could keep my balance long enough to stand on the top pole, my fingers would still be about twenty inches short.

I had the impulse to set myself carefully, then leap. Just the thought of it made me tremble. Then below, where the sleek ironstone gave way to the softer sand-stone, I saw another of the small, funnel-like holes apparently worn by dripping water.

When I understood what I would have to do, I began shaking all over again. I could think of no other way. I did what little shaping I had to do with the pick; not too much, for the fit had to be tight.

Then I gathered my strength, listening to the sharp, rasping pant of my breath. Once I started making this last move, I would have to work rapidly. Huddling there, I could find some illusion of safety. I didn't want to move. I guess my shoulders must have sagged even more. It didn't seem as if the ache could ever leave them.

I began thinking of other things I had done. Mostly my thoughts tended to concentrate on Vena's and my year in the wilderness. Even though at best this present adventure could only mean a final end to all that, it was the pleasantness of the memories that gave me heart for what I had to do.

Bracing myself once more, I reached carefully downward and lifted the lower pole. One end of it implanted firmly in the makeshift socket. The wood slanted upward like a stubby flagpole. The next moment I was shinnying up it.

My head broke through the vegetation. I had my arms on solid ground. Then I was up. I was scrambling back from the edge. I was stretching flat on the blessed ground, while my heart slowed its high, hard thumping. Bushman was running from where the horses were picketed, a short distance away, and then he was licking my face.

I was so drenched with perspiration that the coldness in the wind quickly made itself felt. Too, there was Vena, and although everything was under control now, there was still a lot to be done. I crawled cautiously back through the tangle of highbush cranberries, wild roses, and willow that masked the opening.

It didn't take long once I had the entrance clearer. The lariat I carried on my saddle, plus the manila rope we'd brought for lashing down the fossil we'd hoped to collect, provided ample line for Vena to tie around herself so I could support her up out of the shaft.

The last few feet, past the rim of smooth rock where

she could no longer help herself, were the hardest. Then I had both hands on her, and I was dragging her into the wonderfully bright, sweet, beautiful sunlight.

20

The Woods, The Cabin,
The Girl

"I'd like for us to climb Bullhead," she said again. "Wouldn't you like that?"

"Of course, I'd like it," I said. "I've always wanted to climb Bullhead. But I want it to be entirely up to you. There are still a couple of hours of daylight left, and if we keep to the open ridges until we get east of Bull Creek, we can be back at the cabin tonight."

We kept looking at each other.

"It isn't as though we can't come back up here to King Gething's some other time if we want," I said, "and climb Bullhead then."

"When would that be?"

"I don't know," I told her finally, and she looked away.

"There's one thing I learned underground," she said when her eyes came back, "and that's not to put off living. I kept thinking of all sorts of things I'd wanted to do but had put off, and I kept wondering if we'd ever have another chance."

"All right," I said, and the more I thought about it, the better I liked the idea. "Let's stay over and climb Bullhead in the morning."

Vena rested her head on my shoulder for a moment, and her hands tightened behind my neck.

"Thank you," she said.

"For what?" I asked. "I'm the one who's always wanted to go up Bullhead."

"I have, too," she said, "but that isn't what I mean." I guess I must have looked uncertain.

"For letting me share your dream, Brad, and for helping me to love it, too. For everything, darling."

The river stretched below us the next morning like a vast chain, rusty with sunrise light. The jam in Box Canyon must have broken sometime during the night, for I remembered awakening with a renewed roaring in my ears, and now there was the constant glitter of ice cakes, like moving links between winter and spring.

Bushman's barking lifted about us as we neared the first line of cliffs on the slope above the mine buildings. We'd left him tied near the horses, not because of porcupines for he has shown elaborate disdain for these ever since his last experience here, but because we were afraid he might get hurt trying to scale the rocks. He'd be all right where he was, and we'd left an explanatory note in case King Gething should return.

Already the country was opening before us, as if some inducement was necessary to spur us higher. By keeping to the edge of the canyon upriver from the one in which King had located his mining operation, we climbed the first few lines of rocks where they were least steep. Then we recrossed the narrowing slope and descended partway down the side of the first chasm to get over the next precipices where they were most gradual.

All sorts of small things seemed to be happening that made us happy, and although we had to pause frequently to catch our breaths and to surmount obstructions, nothing seemed as important as the fact that we were together, and safe, and finally well on our way up the mountain that had so long been beckoning.

The wind had a wild free whistle to it as it surged across the rocks and among the stunted undergrowth. My palms enjoyed the smooth, warm surface of a granite outcrop. Suddenly, the complexities of modern life seemed a long way off. Here on the mountainside, it was as though we were first arrivals, a part of an orderly and harmonious existence as rightfully as night and day.

There was freedom about it all, a release that left part of my mind free and allowed all sorts of nearly forgotten things to come back into it. At least, I had supposed them forgotten because I hadn't thought of them for weeks. But there they were: that walk along the Esplanade in the snow when I was finally deciding to come to the woods, the old man in the theatre, and the expression on Vena's face in the candle-lit restaurant on Newbury Street when she had agreed to marry me and to try wilderness living for a year.

Well, now the year was up, and soon we would be heading back. I wondered if it would be possible to find another apartment on Gloucester Street or in that general part of the Back Bay, and I wondered about making a living. Our expenses would be astronomically higher than they were now, and with all the interruptions, I wouldn't have nearly as much time for writing. The more we try to govern time, I thought, the more it rules us.

Our friends, the ones who'd noticed we had been away, would be asking how the year had been, and I began wondering how I could answer them. The most noticeable thing on the mountainside right now was the wind. All of a sudden, it seemed like the breath of the passing year.

I didn't want to think any more. The best thing seemed to be to pick a goal and to concentrate every effort on climbing toward it. What must have been a solitary drop of dew was flashing among some lichen above us. Acting like a prism, it was gleaming like a sapphire. A few steps higher and I could see the same spot shining like an emerald. I had to keep my eye on it and to climb in exactly the right line, and then, all of a sudden, it had transformed into a topaz.

"Can we," Vena was calling, "can we rest for just a moment?"

"Of course," I said. Then I found I was out of breath, too. "I'm sorry."

"It's all right," she said. "All at once, you seemed in such a rush."

"I guess it seemed as if life was rushing by," I said. "I'm sorry."

"It's all right," she said again. "It's just that it gave me a sort of funny feeling to be left behind."

The easiest way to proceed seemed to be to drop into the top of King's canyon, now only a shallow declivity, and to ascend its farther side. Frost began appearing beneath the scant clumps of brush, like white shadows not yet run off by the thin rays of the advancing sun. A tall clump of dead grass was a yellowish white, tipped with frost that dissolved into blinding sparkles as the sun touched it.

Beside me, Vena slipped on the slope. I caught her elbow, and then I was sprawling, too.

"You didn't hurt yourself, did you?" I asked her anxiously.

"No, I'm fine. It's just that it's so nice and soft," She drew a deep breath. "I hate to move."

"We'd better move as far as that rock, though."

"We don't have to stop at all unless you want to," she said, sitting up quickly.

"It isn't that," I said. "It's just that it's pretty soggy right here. This must be where King's creek starts."

The smell of the morass, mysterious somehow, lifted about us as we sat on a granite outcrop and looked northward at the gleaming spine of the Butler Range. The stirring odor of the peat bog in the making, strengthening with the season as increasing warmth stimulated the bacteria of decomposition, seemed to bring me closer to the steamy beginning of things where the first germs of life had stirred.

This must be a remnant, I thought, of that older swampland where the dinosaurs had roamed, and it was as if those cells of my most primitive ancestors still deep within me were being moved by the memory. It seemed all at once eminently fitting that all this, the very enigma of creation, should remain cradled near the crest of the mountain that, ever since our arrival, had always held such a particular lure for me.

The morning fell behind us as we climbed. Helping one another, we worked our way higher, now slanting westward again. Finally, we were on a narrow end of the rough dome. Below on the opposite slope, among sheer precipices that dropped toward the old river mine far beneath, white shapes were bunched.

"Mountain goat," I said.

I thought she would be excited, because she usually reacted more swiftly than I do to anything new and novel. Instead, she only gave the goats a brief look, then glanced around her.

"Oh," she said. Then she asked if this was the top.

"No, I think it's back toward the head of that canyon beyond King's." I felt vaguely disappointed. "See those huge blocks of rocks? That looks the highest."

"Yes," she said, but only part of her seemed to be answering. "It does, doesn't it?"

"Let's go up there," I said, "when you're ready."

She nodded and started off so abruptly that I caught her hand.

"I didn't mean there was any rush, Vena. You're not getting too tired, are you?"

"No," she said, "I feel wonderful."

"After all," I said, "yesterday probably took a lot more out of both of us than we realize."

"Maybe it helped me see a lot of things more clearly, too. I'm mixed up these days. Anyway, all this," and she spread her arms, "makes it right again. This is one reason why I wanted to get on top of Bullhead after being beneath it."

"Well, if you're sure you're all right," I said. I waited for her to go on, but she remained silent. "Or if you'd rather, we could have our lunch right here."

"Anywhere will be wonderful, Brad. I was just thinking, that's all." Her eyes met mine, and then she seemed to look about her for the first time. "Let's do climb to the top first."

She swung my hand in hers. Somehow, it was as if she had just caught up with me again, although as far as I was concerned, we had never been apart. However, now that she was surely back once more, I found my mind wandering to such prosaic thoughts as had either of the horses got a foot over a halter shank, and what was Bushman doing at the end of his leash, and was everything all right back at our cabin. Then we were on the edge of the largest of the rocks, with the whole country stretching out before us.

There was Fort St. John where that first day our truck had turned west toward the mountains and Hudson Hope. The Peace River, miles of it, rippled with sparkling silver. Chinaman Lake, where last year we had refound spring, was a white gleam to the north. In nearly the opposite direction was the glare of the frozen lake behind the ridge, across from the cabin, where Vena had discovered her first wild vegetables.

It was an exquisite moment, a victory without the destruction of anything except self-doubt. Nothing, I suddenly felt all the more strongly, can bring one peace but oneself.

Everything, the distances and the view and the fact that not a thing was about us now but the wild free wind, brought a sense of release in space. This, in turn, gave me a feeling of detachment in time. It was as though, from such a vantage point, I should be able to see, too, the future I had not even lived.

When we got back down to the clearing, shadows from the encircling woods were closing in on the mine buildings. Bushman was barking, and the horses

seemed glad to see us, also, but there was still no sign
of King.

"Well, we made it," I said. "It took longer to come
down than I thought it would."

"Will it be all right to let Bushman loose now?"

"Yes, he'll be fine. He hasn't even got close to a
porcupine since tangling with those two on his last trip
here. That was a pretty drastic lesson."

"Maybe," Vena said, "all of us need a drastic lesson
first."

She seemed about to go on, and then she stopped.

"How much daylight is left, Brad?"

"Oh, a couple of hours," I told her. "Do you want to
start getting us something to eat while I water the
horses?"

"You'll think I'm foolish, but yesterday you said we
could ride home from here in two hours. That's what
I'd really like to do. Can we go home, Brad?"

"Sure we can, if that's what you really want." I tried
to rearrange my thinking, but I found I couldn't concentrate. "Vena, what's the matter?"

She had been staring up the slope we had just descended, and now, when her eyes fell again to mine,
they looked startled.

"Why, nothing."

"Something's bothering you. The last day or so particularly, you've been driving yourself."

"Please don't worry about me," she said. "You've
been worrying about me all day. What's unnatural
about wanting to be back home?"

I wasn't worried exactly, but I did find myself getting a little impatient, for all this was so memorable
that I wanted her to enjoy it with me. I went back over
the time we had known each other and tried to remember if she had ever acted this way before. What I
recalled was that difficult period when we had been
trying to break away from the city. For awhile it had
seemed that I might have to start off by myself, and

although then the idea was that she would join me later, until it was all settled she had driven herself much the same way.

Then saddling and packing occupied my thoughts. We were loping back down the mine road again with Bushman racing ahead, alongside, and behind. I pulled in Chinook after about a mile, and Cloud slowed, too. But both horses continued to step out and occasionally to break into a trot. We reached Larry Gething's old trapping cabin at the right of the road. Both horses seemed a little hesitant when we neck-reined them past the partially toppled logs. Then we were on the open ridge just beyond, and once more they picked up their gait.

The stream that eventually became Dancing Falls wound somewhere beneath us. Now that the warmth of the sunshine was ebbing from the chilling air, a current of mist was starting to twine above the water, marking its course.

We crossed the neck of the high flat below which, on the Peace, Vena had lit her first campfire and we had eaten our first trail meal. Then we were on another open ridge, this one circling the beginnings of Bull Creek which was tracing its presence, too, with long, slow ribbons of vapor. Far to our right, the wider stretches of the Peace River were taking up the light the sky was losing.

Bullhead loomed high beside us, and I was a little sorry to be leaving it so soon. But after all, it wasn't as though Bullhead wouldn't still be here, waiting for me. It was inconceivable that I would not be back one day, if only for a few months, when the noisy confusion of the city again became too stifling.

I hoped that Vena would feel the same way. I hoped that no conflict about the respective merits of wilderness and civilization would build up between us, with each of our natures straining a different way, and I wondered if she'd considered the possibility of such a growing difference, too. She had, I supposed, for she always thought of everything.

"Would you like to rest?" I asked her now.

"No, but let's walk and lead the horses awhile," she said. "It's magnificent up here, isn't it? I wish we could see Bullhead from the cabin."

A breeze came from the ravine, carrying with it the rush of the river and a sweet damp scent, and Vena's dark brown hair blew across her forehead.

"We head right along the rim here," I said. "There's ice under some of this kinnikinic, so you'd better watch where you're going."

But, then, she was always watching where she went.

A velvet bulge of darkness was pushing up from the gorges and the thick spruce swamps below us. Clouds massing around Bullhead exhaled the soft luminescence of twilight. A long fragile hedge of wind-trellised cumulus clouds above the river bloomed with such color that even the darkening sides of Rocky Mountain Canyon seemed to glow with lilacs, violets, and a deep purple that was almost fluorescent.

The day was going, and never in our lives, I thought, would there be another like it. Blue, of an opulence I couldn't remember ever having seen before, drenched the last flaring embers of the cloud-smoking sunset. In the north, the Aurora Borealis started to sketch its vaguenesses in silver. A yellow roundness of moon floated higher in the east.

The thud of the horses' hoofs, Bushman's occasional rushes through the bush, and the small noises of our own feet leaped out against the sudden soundlessness. It was as if the north was slowly and silently inhaling. Then it started letting out its breath just as gently, as if the sheer weight of the darkness was almost too much to be moved. Again, I could hear a breeze starting to stir the trees.

"We don't require very much in life, do we?" Vena's

voice startled me. "It takes something like the last few days to make one see how, actually, half the confusion in the world comes from not realizing how few things we really need. That's one thing, at least, the woods have taught me."

"It's a pretty important thing," I answered. "Most people are so busy thinking of what they lack that they don't take time to appreciate what they have. I suppose that one tendency has caused more misery than all the wars in history."

"It's pretty easy to do," she said. "I've almost done it myself more than once. Is this where we head down?"

"This is it," I said. "Watch your step."

Although I could see the game trail perfectly well, the flat below seemed dark and distant. It was a strange sensation because stars seemed to be hanging low all across the woods. Even during the primitive years of the Cretaceous Sea, I thought, the stars had not shone as brightly, for then the steaming vegetation had been giving off continuous vapors that had obscured the warm and humid air.

I heard some change in the tempo of the sounds behind me. When I turned, stepping aside to avoid Chinook who had the habit of walking on my heels, I saw Vena had stopped and was standing beside her saddle.

"If you don't mind walking a little bit further," I said, "I don't think I'd get on just yet. We'll be down on the flat in a few more yards."

"I was just hooking my stirrups over the saddle horn," Vena replied. "They were catching on the bushes. I don't mind walking."

"Fine," I said. "There's the flat just below. I think the best way will be to go across Bull Creek and to come to the cabin along the river bank."

"I'm not in any hurry," she said, and she sounded more relaxed than she had for a long while. "Isn't this a beautiful night? I don't think I've ever seen such a beautiful night."

"I'm not in any hurry, either," I said, "but it will be lighter that way."

It was a beautiful night. I was glad we were sharing it, that we'd always have it to remember.

I'd meant for us to resume riding once we'd reached the level. First though, there was Bull Creek to cross. Because of the soft banks here, this was easier to do afoot. Then there was the possibility of riding into an unseen branch. What we did when we got among the open poplars was to loop Cloud's halter shank around the horn of Chinook's saddle. That way Vena and I could walk together. It seemed right on such a night to be walking together.

A quiet bulking of shadows appeared ahead.

"There's the cabin," I said.

"I'll help you put up the horses, Brad."

"You don't have to."

"I'd like to, I don't want to go in yet."

Bushman began barking when the horses, unsaddled at last and in their corral, started rolling. Then he stopped.

"Brad," Vena said, "tell me one thing. Do I have to stay in the woods?"

"No, of course, you don't," I said. "It's still the same as we agreed. I thought you understood that. We'll begin packing tomorrow."

I saw her face, white and hazy in the stillness.

"This may sound foolish," she said, "but I suppose it's sort of how walking is easy when you're leading a horse. As long as we don't have to stay, I don't want to go back."

"Vena," I began, and then I stopped.

"Yes?"

"It's not just because of me?" I said, "You can't mean that you really want to stay?"

"After all this, how could I ever go back? I mean, really go all the way back? Could you, Brad?"

"Why," I answered, "that's what I've been expecting to do all along."

"It would be as if we were only half-living, don't you see?" she asked. "Part of you would always be here. Part of me would be here, too. You understand that, don't you, darling?"

"Maybe I've always understood it," I said.

"I think I've always known it, too. That must be why I've been so difficult and rebellious."

"Why, you haven't been that way at all."

"Yes, I have, from the very first," she said. "Only it's been mostly myself I've been fighting. I suppose it was because I was afraid of losing my identity. Maybe that fear was stronger in me because up to now I've had to fight for everything all my life."

Her hands found mine and held them tight.

"Only I can see now that the place where there's really a danger of being swallowed up is in the city, not here where each of us really needs the other, now and always."

Bushman was barking again. I realized that the murmur of migrating birds, winging northward free as air, was pressing rousingly against the night. Hoarse throats were tossing their impulsive chatter back and forth across the drowsing wilderness, singly and in a swelling chorus. Then there was the nearing surge of wings.

Where the hot smudge of the moon was melting away the blackness, I made out an uneven angle of wild swan. One of them seemed to dislodge a star, and the star fell toward the hidden top of Bullhead Mountain.

Even after the birds had disappeared upriver, I still seemed to be following their strange, compulsive passage—until it became a dimly remembered shadow, centuries deep in my consciousness. It was strange in a way because I had never felt more alive.

"Don't bother to stop on the way back," I called after them, starting with Vena toward our cabin. "We're both where we belong."